T0114882

THE INTRIGUING
Phenomena
BEYOND THE
Cross

Dr Patrick Nyamadzi (PhD)

WESTBOW
PRESS®
A DIVISION OF THOMAS NELSON
& ZONDERVAN

This book is a work of non-fiction. Unless otherwise noted, the author and the publisher make no explicit guarantees as to the accuracy of the information contained in this book and in some cases, names of people and places have been altered to protect their privacy.

WestBow Press books may be ordered through booksellers or by contacting:

WestBow Press
A Division of Thomas Nelson & Zondervan
1663 Liberty Drive
Bloomington, IN 47403
www.westbowpress.com
844-714-3454

Because of the dynamic nature of the Internet, any web addresses or links contained in this book may have changed since publication and may no longer be valid. The views expressed in this work are solely those of the author and do not necessarily reflect the views of the publisher, and the publisher hereby disclaims any responsibility for them.

Any people depicted in stock imagery provided by Getty Images are models, and such images are being used for illustrative purposes only. Certain stock imagery © Getty Images.

Scripture taken from the King James Version of the Bible.

ISBN: 978-1-6642-0450-8 (sc)
ISBN: 978-1-6642-0451-5 (e)

Print information available on the last page.

WestBow Press rev. date: 09/16/2020

CONTENTS

AUTHOR'S PREFACE

The purpose of this book is to give a believer the knowledge of the Bible, Christ, the indwelling Spirit as the focus. It is intended to stimulate the reader's desire to know more about Christ with His unsearchable, inexhaustible, immeasurable and incomprehensible treasures and riches to the saints. This is a scholarly collated documentation concerning the incarnate, resurrected and ascended Christ, the Spirit and His finished works. This is also, essentially, a crystallized and compressed choreograph of the eternal mind of God from eternity past, present and eternity future. I am endeavouring to challenge the reader to migrate from the periphery of interpretation and understanding of the Bible to the epicentre. Deep calls unto deep. We need to drink from deep waters as the water tables are rising. This edition, I believe, it is an intellectually and spiritually captivating adventure. Into this massive, gigantic and ginormous spiritual infrastructure called ***THE CHRIST, (the Khristos) which is also an intriguing universal and corporate personality.***

It is my sincere hope and trust that in reading this book, you should experience a multiplicity of spiritual manifestations at the level of your faith. The multi-dimensionalities and multi-layeredness of Christ has to become a tangible reality through His Spirit and the Word. However, it is important to note that our faith walk is not like a leisure stroll in the park hence the urgent need for us to engage the Spirit for the demonstration and manifestation of His power. This should then strengthen and anchor our faith. It is, I believe, God's deepest desire to see the transitioning of believers from the outer court mentality to the Holy of Holies mind set as typologically presented in the study of the tabernacle of Moses in Exodus 25. Maturity is the gateway to heir-ship and it is in essence God's ultimate goal. Let us then therefore study and navigate the truth in the word together. God has enveloped Himself in His **Word**. His Word is self-validating, and self-revealing. Therefore, I believe it is practically impossible to interface with the **WORD** and remain at the same position under the same condition. The supernaturality and eternality in the Word makes it efficacious to transform humanity to its original state. For His Sabbath (satisfaction) May this God through His Christ the Spirit continuously give you refreshed, energized spiritual and mental faculties to pursue the treasure in **HIS ETERNAL WORD, CHRIST.** Our GOD is faithful to the end. Remember Proverbs *10 v 7 "....The memory of the righteous is blessed........"Proverbs 24v5......a man of knowledge increase strength ...*

ACKNOWLEDGEMENTS

This work is not an overnight individual compilation of theological or academic data but it is a synergistic product of various minds in the academic community. I am profoundly grateful to the inspiration and wisdom of a number of great men and women of God who passionately laboured to release the potential in me. Indeed, they motivated me and this is definitely an unquestionable legacy to my generation. I am undoubtedly convinced that I am the confirmation of Isaiah 60 v15 *thee* in which God said ',.........*I will make an eternal excellency, and become a joy to many generations.* 'I believe my indelible footprints of faith walk will be traced through this work.

I am also grateful to the members, friends and colleagues at Faith Ministries Zimbabwe. Their faithful prayers, patience and love inspired me to partly fulfil my purpose and unleash my potential.

For the development and production of this book, I emotionally feel a profound sense of gratitude to:

My wonderful wife, Sophia and our children particularly my daughter Shumirai who laboured tirelessly in editing this book. Also I extend special thanks to my son Tendai and my sister Kudakwashe for financial support. Claudine Madzinga the Administrator for HIS MERCY CHRISTIAN INSTITUTE she spent hours typing and proof reading this book. What an awesome work? I greatly appreciate.

My close circle friends, pastors and board members for His Mercy

Christian College. My friend Pastor Dr Walter Senah a scholar par excellence, Dr. Kames Mabvundwi friend and Board Member of HMCC Dr. Phillips Andrews, Dr. Stephen Fletcher. Dr. Moreen Kent and Dr. Tobby Awasu President of Omega International.

Finally, I am grateful and forever extend my thanks to the source and supplier of all potential, the Omni-potent one Father, the Lord of all creation and His Son, my elder Brother Jesus Christ and my personal counsellor, the Holy Spirit. Thanks for the privilege of serving you in a more intimate, executive, kingly and priestly way.

INTRODUCTION

"Information is abundant but the understanding of it is scarce"
Professor Hamilton Hub

Throughout my research as a scholar innumerable academic materials have passed through my hands. Materials ranging from philosophy, theology and a varied range in social sciences. I have come to the realisation that in the depth of every human soul, on earth is a search for meaning of purpose, significance and value. This is regardless of any racial, cultural, religious and social background. There is an insatiable desire in man to search for answers to existence. There is an internal search common among all humankind. Throughout my research I became aware of many disparate views of theology and even philosophy. With my chronic heathenistic and neo-liberal religious background the message of the cross of Jesus Christ brought an undeniable divine turnaround to my life. But after a period of time associating with, the charismatic and evangelical movements my life was shrouded with more questions than answers in a number of theological issues relating the Christian faith. The message of the cross was and is still being exhaustively preached to us in churches. Thanks be to God for the transformative effect of the cross. Though it should be highlighted that we are delivered by the cross but we do not worship or idolise the symbol of the cross. With all the theological knowledge on the message of the cross it appeared a huge and yet to be explained gulf was created in me, hence the desire and zeal to investigate and interrogate the phenomena beyond the cross. This book is about the fundamentals of the Christian faith and is relevant for Christ students in, theo-academics, any aspiring New Testament ministers of the gospel of Jesus Christ and even researchers. It does not, however, provide psychological motivational handles neither quick-fix solutions to the problems of this life.. In this book I believe by God's grace I have endeavoured to provide a condensed and crystallised revelation of Christ in His glorified state primarily from the New Testament perspective the growth of a believer in Christ.

An in-depth analysis and panoramic view on the events which transpired after the cross are availed. **What happened after the cross? What are the doctrinal implications of the events that happened after crucifixion? Should Christians focus on the cross only in teaching the Bible?** These theological questions and many more intriguing questions are addressed in this book. Most bible readers have a tendency to view what it says through their own cultural and life circumstances. This can happen almost subconsciously as we read the text e.g. when most people in the church read about the thief on the cross, they think immediately of a burglar that held up a store or broke into a home. They may be surprised to learn that the guy was actually a Jewish revolutionary figure who was part of the growing movement in Palestine eager to overthrow Roman rule. Therefore, an accurate historical contextual analysis is vital to bring out the proper meaning of events in scripture.

In my constant interaction with a number of Bible enthusiasts and apologetics I have noticed that biblical literature is one of the most misunderstood literature possibly because of the supernatural qualities associated with it. There are a lot of noticeable interpretative distortions in the present day church which are tantamount to violently disfiguring the Holy Scriptures and ignoring the divine tutelage of the Holy Ghost John 16:13-15, *"Howbeit when he, the Spirit of truth, is come, he will guide you into all truth: for he shall not speak of himself; but whatsoever he shall hear, that shall he speak: and he will shew you things to come. All things that the Father hath are mine: therefore said I, that he shall take of mine, and shall shew it unto you.*"

No doubt there is a need in the church for learning and studying more about the WORD of God, particularly more focused on the New Testament theology. Relevant historical and cultural insights provide an added dimension to the existing biblical perspectives on the resurrected Christ

The motivation for writing this book came from the discovery of the knowledge gap particularly on the events that happened after the crucifixion of Jesus Christ. More interestingly the universal impact of His resurrection, ascension, descension as the Spirit and His ultimate enthronement as the King and the Lord of Glory.

My deepest heart cry is that the entire body of Christ should come to the knowledge of Jesus Christ like Apostle Paul cried in Romans 10:1-2, *"Brethren, my heart's desire and prayer to God for Israel is that they might be saved. For I bear them record that they have a zeal of God, but not according to knowledge."* Paul cried for Israel, but I cry for nations to come to the Lordship of Jesus Christ for life. Many times in the past we have stressed that the Bible covers two main matters, i.e. Christ and the Church. However, from another angle, the bible is a book of life and building. Christ is life and the church is a building. With knowledge and understanding believers partake Christ as their inheritance to build God's kingdom. This is, fundamentally, God's eternal purpose from eternity past. The eternal purpose of God in Christ is the hub, a massive universal wheel in a wheel as illustrated by Ezekiel's vision in chapter 1:16, "*.....**a wheel in the middle of wheel**"* His will and purpose in Christ should prevail. Our destiny in Christ is articulately defined in His WORD. It is my sincere hope that any believing reader of this book will have a new or added perspective of the Christ of our God. Philemon 6, "**That the communication of thy faith may become effectual by the acknowledging of every good thing which is in you in Christ Jesus.**" We need to acknowledge and appreciate that which is deposited in us. We, either individually or corporately must be revealed as the sons of God. Dr. Catharina said, "*We are the conduit to bring heaven to earth*" I believe this statement is accurate and should ignite our passion and desire to pursue Christ. We are expected to be the manifestation of the realities of Christ.

One

Beyond the Cross

"There is glory in what I do not know, so my pursuit is in the discovery of what I do not know" Professor W. Bukupa

"Can Christian faith survive if resurrection and ascension of Christ is dismissed as fables of mythology" Dr. Hubert Kant

"...to the Lamb that was slain from the foundation of the world" Revelation 13:8.

"My people are destroyed for lack of knowledge ...." Hosea 4:6

"The ox knows its owner and the donkey his masters crib but my people (Israel) do not know and have no knowledge." Isaiah 1:3

"If the clouds are full of rain they empty themselves upon the earth ....." Ecclesiastes 11:3

"....... A man of knowledge increase in strength" Proverbs 24:5

".....through knowledge shall the just be delivered ......" Proverbs 11:9

"......may give unto you the Spirit of wisdom and revelation in the knowledge of him" Ephesians 1:17

In the academic world we believe that there is no individual with monopoly of knowledge and the acknowledgement of one having the deficiency of it is the beginning of learning. In the academia, it is said knowledge is power but post-modernist scholars widely believe that learning is the superpower. Therefore, learning must be an intentional

1

goal for every believer. We believe that it is only Jesus Christ who is the sole custodian of all knowledge Colossians 1:17, *"And he is before all things and by him all things consist"*. **Beyond and outside Christ there is no knowledge to discover.** Colossians 2:3, *"Christ is the epitome and embodiment of knowledge."* Christ is the centrality, circumference and universality of who God is. The pursuit of Christ is therefore the pursuit of -knowledge.

Over the years in our early Christian walk we mainly hear messages on the cross, repentance from sins, the must be "born again theology" the message on eschatology that is, on end of the age. Well this is good and exciting as it creates a sense of hope and assurance for the future. However, as the ministration of the Spirit continued, an insatiable hunger for the knowledge of Christ increased and more questions were stirred up in me. I could have questions like, "I am born again so now what? Is it the end? Can there be more?" If I die today what will happen? I would go to the church and listen to the same message on "carrying the cross" over and over again. Believers are encouraged to carry the cross. Without carrying the cross no guarantee for heaven. Regular confession for sins was emphasised. For me the thought of missing heaven was untenable, for assurance, then I could work hard on the confession processions. This was tedious and, tiring. The truth is, as I now know, legalism and traditionalism can be a yoke. This is why Jesus cried in Matthew 11v28 *"....Come unto me, all ye that labour and are heavily burdened I will give you rest v29 Take my yoke...........which is easier and lighter"*. When praying before kneeling down we were told to confess our sins lest prayers are not answered. Always we were told of the danger to live and die in sin. Hell, hell was the reminder week in week out. Though I believed to would have been saved I lived a life controlled by sin consciousness, fear, inferiority complex and confusion. I virtually suffered from spiritual stagnation, lethargy mediocrity, docility and lukewarmness due to ignorance. I had no assurance of my salvation in Christ. I would be born again and born again every Sunday this was deadly ignorance.

After a couple of years I realised the need to search and understand the Word on redemption, as provided by God in Christ. The voyage to search for the truth started. I remember in Church one Sunday one pastor preached on the crucifixion of Jesus. Whaa, whaa what an emotional historical narrative it was. The torture, the humiliation, the blood, nails on the cross were graphically narrated. To me the question still remained "why the cross". Why would God allow such a treacherous, bloody and scandalous act to happen in His sight? Was there no other way than the excruciating pain of the cross? However, having gathered so much knowledge in biblical literature, I was still not satisfied, the subject of the cross remained a mystery to me. The cross still remained an intriguing phenomenon which implored for a rigorous theological inquiry. Even past and contemporary philosophers and Bible scholars have not fully answered this question. 1 Corinthians 1:18 *"For the preaching of the cross is to them that perish foolishness; but unto us which are saved it is the power of God."* 1 Corinthians 1:27 *"But God hath chosen the foolish things of the world to confound the wise; and God hath chosen the weak things of the world to confound the things which are mighty.* The cross was and still is the highest terrain for God to demonstrate His wisdom to His creation. One writer said," **the act of the cross is far beyond human comprehension and should only be appreciated from the perspective of its effect on humanity".**

Actually, interestingly, one day the Holy Spirit flashed in my spirit an image of the importance of Information Computer Technology (ICT). Though I am a novice to ICT, I could relate. It was like a whisper in my ears. Do you know that Pentecost, the lavish outpouring of the Holy Spirit on humanity facilitated the universal accessibility of God by man? A "divine WI-FI" was made available to all man. I started relating to the function of the internet. It was a strikingly illuminating picture. I appreciated the Holy Spirit, the teacher who uses life changing skills to communicate. John 16:13. He uses pictures, symbols, parables, numbers etc. Essentially, the Holy Spirit helps us to connect or communicate with the Father in heaven through His Son Jesus Christ. Though the Father dwells in us subjectively but he objectively dwells in His fullness of glory in the heavens. This is a mystery. I remember what Dr Hutzell said, **"Christ is like a monolithic, massive infrastructure of a universal internet server.** Whosoever believe in Him can access the divine pass word is **ONLY BELIEVE?** What a thought -provoking insight. With my rudimentary knowledge in ICT I could relate. Using WI-FI (symbolically the Holy Spirit) you can visit different sites on this internet (symbolically Christ). In relation to Christ and our fellowship with the Father, Christ has a multiple "inexhaustible sites" Colossians 2:3 *"In whom are hid all the treasures of wisdom and knowledge."* Essentially, for us to grow in the knowledge of Him we need to constantly "log in" and visit as many "sites" as possible in Him. This essentially created the motivation to write this edition- **"The INTRIGUING Phenomena Beyond the Cross"**

With several years involved with the evangelical movements, I have discovered a knowledge gap hence the desire to research more. *Most preachers only focus on the cross; and the fundamentals of salvation, therefore they dwell on the same site, the "cross website" forever ignoring and disadvantaging themselves in accessing and understanding the multi-dimensionalities and multi-grainedness of this extensively gigantic, ginormous and inexhaustible spiritual infrastructure called Christ.* The entire redemptive drama has to be interrogatively studied in the context of its multiple aspects namely the mystery of incarnation, human living, resurrection, ascension, glorification, exaltation, enthronement, and the descension of Christ as Spirit on Pentecost. What about Christ as the mystery of the church? What about what happened after crucifixion? Hence, the theological voyage in searching for a detailed account and revelation on this Christ.

The expectation is therefore for all believers to migrate to maturity. For sonship and **heirship.** *Sonship is a position which gives us an entitlement for inheritance. Position issues possession. From this understanding we realise that possession should follow position.*

4

Our destiny must be defined by appreciating our position in Christ not possessions. God does not expect a Christian to remain in the state of mediocrity, passivity and stereotype, lingering around the periphery of the structures of Christ but advance to the epicentre. Arch Bishop Lubert talks of **"the forever outer court believers"**. They never endeavour or desire to migrate to maturity and Son-ship. Yes, we must talk and study about the cross and the Passover but we need to move on to feast of the Pentecost and Tabernacles. The Holy of Holies where intimacy is established and this is the ultimate and desired goal of the Father.

We now realise that revelation is progressive, dynamic and transformative. It is God's desire and pleasure to be known by man in a more intimate and passionate way. In studying the bible our primary objective and aim is to know him through Christ. In Philippians 3:10, *"That I may know him and power of his resurrection ...."* Also the same Apostle in I Corinthians 2:2 we hear him *"For I determined not to know everything among you save Jesus Christ and him crucified."* Galatians 4:9, *"But now after that ye have known God or rather are known of God ......"* We find out from these scriptures the central emphasis is on knowing. We are a product of what we know and our capacity to benefit from the redemptive work of Christ is principally dependant on the level of knowledge we have. But we thank God for the outpouring of the Holy Spirit who is the Chief educator and His divine tutelage and mentorship is embodied in the revelation and knowledge of Christ.

We realise that as we endeavour to know God, our minds are finite and we have limited capacity to grasp the full knowledge about God. In fact, to be more precise, we as humans will never understand God in His fullness. However, we believe, God because of His infinite, dimensionless and immeasurable love for man, He has sovereignly chosen to allow a certain component (part) of Himself to be known by man. God is truly incomprehensible, incomparable and immeasurable but amazingly knowable. To be more precise and direct, His incomprehensibility transcends His knowability.

He remains incomprehensible but can be known to us to a certain extent. It is the revelation through the Holy Ghost that He "slices" a portion of Himself to be known by humans. Like the scripture says in Ezekiel 20 v5 *".........I made myself known to them ...."* and many other related scriptural references in the Bible. The intention of this book therefore is to explain certain components of the truth about God which has been veiled from believers for generations, as we mainly focus on studying the post- crucifixion phenomena (events).

John 2:2-8, *"And both Jesus was called, and his disciples, to the marriage. And when they wanted wine, the mother of Jesus saith unto him, they have no wine. Jesus saith unto her, Woman, what have I to do with thee? Mine hour is not yet come. His mother saith unto the servants, whatsoever he saith unto you, do it. And there were set there six waterpots of stone, after the manner of the purifying of the Jews, containing two or three firkins apiece. Jesus saith unto them, Fill the waterpots with water. And they filled them up to the brim. And he saith unto them, Draw out now, and bear unto the governor of the feast. And they bare it."* This was the first miracle by Jesus in His entry to ministry and the initial manifestation of Himself as the incarnate Jesus who had appeared to redeem mankind. This was God incognito. They did not know that Jesus was Jehovah, God who had manifested Himself. Jesus turned water to wine, what an amazing miracle. Tradition, has it that weddings that time were so invaluable occasions which immensely represented the Jewish socio-cultural values. Wine was essentially associated with joy and celebration. It was then sadly depressing that the host of this wedding was plunged into an embarrassment and shame culturally. To avert this chaotic incident the mother of Jesus who was assumed to be family friend of the host intervened. With this miracle we see Jesus asserting His intention on the earth that is to, bring abundant joy to this desperate world. He did not even pray but gave a simple instruction verse 7, *"Fill the waterpots with water".* It happens to us sometimes we miss God by failing to take simple instruction from the Lord. We always expect God to respond to our challenges in a way which is desirable to us. ***The children of Israel did not expect God to pour manna from heaven***. To them it was strange though they eventually reluctantly partook of it. That simple instructive nagging from within your inner man could be your breakthrough. The interesting part of this miracle is that Jesus said, verse 8, *"Draw out now and bear unto the governor of the feasts"*, verse 10, *"the governor said .... you have kept the good wine until now"*.

I believe God sovereignly has reserved the best wine for this generation. We sincerely appreciate our elders (the generals of faith) in the past generation for their contributions, accomplishments and exploits. But we strongly believe that God is up for new things Isaiah 43:19, ***"Behold, I will do a new thing***; *now it shall spring forth; shall ye not know it? I will even make a way in the wilderness, and rivers in the desert."* He wants to pour out new wine on new wine skins. Mathew 9:16-17, *"No man putteth a piece of new cloth unto an old garment, for that which is put in to fill it up taketh from the garment, and the rest is made worse. Neither do men put new wine into old bottles: else the bottles break, and the wine runneth out, and the bottles perish; but they put new wine into new bottles, and both are preserved."* God is ready to open new frontiers for the saints. Therefore, the church needs to embrace the "sometimes" provocative dynamics of change. The apostolic and prophetic banner is rising in a phenomenal way in heralding the second coming of Christ the Messiah. We are the penultimate generation and God has poured and is still pouring amazing revelations concerning Himself through Christ. We are the generation to enjoy the "best wine". God is upgrading, uplifting, elevating and repositioning the church in preparation of the second coming of the Messiah, His beloved.

As the penultimate generation, the church need to be in tune and alignment with the frequency of the heavenly Christ. God is giving the *governors* (those in the governmental authority to administer in churches) an incredible outpouring and increase of His Spirit. Ecclesiastes 11:3. *"If the clouds are full of rain they empty themselves upon the earth"*. The heavens in Christ are pregnant with revelation knowledge and manifestations of God waiting to be poured on this earth. Like in the days of Moses and the children of Israel in Exodus 14:19. There is a cloud of revelation constantly shifting positions. Saints have to be connected to the move of God. God wants to be known better as the church (the bride) is waiting for the bridegroom (Christ). It is incumbent upon every believer to take deliberate and intentional decision to seek Him more Psalms 42:1, *"As the hart pants for the waterbrooks, so panteth my soul after thee, O God"*. **The water tables are rising to release fresh water** and we have to desire to drink from deep waters.

Seeking God is no longer an option but a priority. As systems of this world continue collapsing we now realise the need for us as a people to seek Him. Psalms 24:6-10, *"This is the generation of them that seek him that seek thy face, O Jacob"* The king of glory is on His way preparing for His coming.

Mathew 6:33, *"But seek ye first the kingdom of God, and his righteousness; and all these things shall be added unto you."* I have come to realise that the more I seek God the more I lose appetite for worldly things. Quite interesting is that the pursuit of worldly pleasure is no longer appealing and Christ has become the centric subject matter. King Solomon in a seemingly disheartening mood said. Ecclesiastes 1:2, *"vanity of vanities saith the preacher vanity of all vanities all is vanity."* We probably need not to get into a detailed explanation of the life of this preacher (Solomon). But the interesting part is when he finally came to end of his life reality dawned on him that this world with its material resources is a waste of time. I personally believe at this stage Solomon was seeing God as the all-fulfilling one What an exciting stage of life. The central message as an encouragement to us is that we need to disassociate ourselves from this materialistic world and give God His space in our lives. Let us hold on that which remain. Hebrews 12:26-28, "I believe in the foundational doctrine of the cross, with its mult-facetedness in definition, essence and functionality. However, we also believe that the message of the cross cannot be complete or absolute without explaining and understanding the other aspects of redemption which includes ascension, exaltation, glorification, enthronement of Christ and even His descension as the Spirit at Pentecost. We need to understand the crowning of Christ as the King of kings in the heavens. This should give us a full panoramic view of the entire redemptive drama. The post-crucifixion events doctrinally if correctly interpreted would build believers in grace and in the knowledge of Christ. The believers understanding of position and identity in Christ is fundamental. and quintessential. Over the years hearing various messages from different platforms I have noticed with concern that most of the messages are centred on the incarnate Christ who had limited expression and influence than the glorified Christ. Essentially, the incarnate Christ is more objective than the glorified Christ. The glorified Christ is more subjective and experiential. We experience Him more in His glorified and ascended state as God. There is need among believers to have a "perspectival adjustment" change of perspectives or paradigm shift in interpreting the Christological aspects of this Christ in God. As we shall see in the epistles of Paul, he articulates in detail the post crucifixion events in a way which should help the believer to discover his or her full redemptive position in Christ. The Pauline epistles give us a clear view of the ascended and glorified Christ, the Spirit. This theological understanding is critical for our spiritual development. This is the word of His grace Acts 20:32, *the word of his grace, which is able to build you up, and to give you an inheritance among all them which are sanctified."*

We need to pursue the knowledge in Christ so that we can correctly represent Him on earth and repel Satan's strategy which is to keep believers in hostage because of ignorance. ***The church should not beautify, glorify, celebrate and decorate biblical illiteracy and ignorance.***

Two

God Has Spoken and is Still Speaking

Hebrews 1:1 *"God who in sundry times and in divers manners spoke in time past unto the fathers by the prophets".*

The undeniable pillar of truth in the Christian faith is the reality of the voice of the Spirit of God. The reality of the indwelling Christ in man. Acts 7:55, *"But he, being full of the Holy Ghost, looked up steadfastly into heaven, and saw the glory of God, and Jesus standing on the right of God".* Jesus' present position at the right hand of the Father is strongly attested in the early Christianity. His exalted position is the fulfilment of Psalm 110:1, *"The LORD said unto my Lord, Sit thou at my right hand, until I make thine enemies thy footstool."* What is unusual here is that Jesus is portrayed as standing not sitting. We are not sure whether what Stephen saw was a Christopheny (the appearing of a form of Christ) or it was a visionary imagination. There have been a variety of theological explanations or schools of thought on this view. Some believe that Jesus stands as the ascended Christ the King and Lord to welcome Stephen; or Jesus rises to make intercession for Stephen. Jesus standing to perform his duties as priest in the heavenly temple. This post-crucifixion phenomenon is intriguing and interesting and as such inevitably stimulates a thought provoking theological inquiry. We can only speculate as to the precise reason why Jesus is standing, but common to all these is the fact that Jesus is actively involved and speaking in response to the needs of his people from his exalted position at the right hand side of the Father. God is speaking and He has spoken. We are the ministers of the Gospel of Christ 1 Corinthians 4:1, *"stewards of the mysteries of God."* I believe when we do ministration even angels write notes on what we are receiving from the Holy Spirit for they do not understand these things. We are an amazing part of creation to them 1 Peter 1:12, *"............ which things the angels desire to look into".* What a privilege we have to be chosen as vessels for the mysteries of the Kingdom. Indeed, this is the abundant grace and love... (1 John 3:1.)

In John's Gospel, Jesus speaks of seeing heaven open and the angels of God ascending and descending on the Son of Man, (John 1:51). This is the imagery of Jacob's ladder (Genesis 28:12). There is divine commerce between heaven and earth with God revealing himself in a new way through His Son. Now Jesus has completed his earthly ministry, heaven is opened again but now the Son of man is essentially in the presence of God watching and involved with his people speaking.

God has spoken and is still speaking "Praise Him". It is absolutely not a small thing that God has spoken and is still speaking. Without speaking God is mysterious. But he has revealed himself in His speaking. *As He is speaking to humanity He desires to speak to people individually* He is no longer mysterious. Now He is the revealed God in Christ. From the Old Testament to the New Testament, He is speaking. The Old Testament is the concealed mystery about Christ and the New Testament is the revealed mystery of Christ. In fact the entire Bible is all about Christ and without Christ there is no God. Essentially, the entire Bible is story of Jesus as the Son of God. Christ is the centrality, circumference and the universality of God. The epicentre of the message of the Bible is Christ, Him crucified, resurrected and ascended. Christ figuratively speaking is **THE LETTER FROM THE ETERNAL** *in contemporary life we know the function of a letter. We realise that the fundamental function of a letter is to* convey a

message of its AUTHOR and a letter displays the character and portrait image of its originator So is JESUS he is the authentic representation of the eternal God. Christ is the letter carrying the message concerning God the Sovereign Father. Precisely, without Christ there is no way we can know GOD. Outside Christ it is vanity to search for God. Any message, which is not focused on Christ is humanistic philosophy and squarely dead religion. Also any message which is centred on the exaltation and elevation of man than Christ is not from God. This is what we find in the Epistle of John, the admonition not to participate in heretic teachings and doctrinally distorted religious practises.

2 John v 7, *"For many deceivers are entered into the world, who confess not that Jesus Christ is come in the flesh. This is a deceiver and an antichrist."* Also 1 John 2:22. The Epistle of 2 John prohibits believers from participating in any heretical teaching concerning Christ's person. In verse 10 the Apostle John says, *"If anyone comes to you and does not bring this teaching do not receive him into your house and do not say to him "Rejoice!"* as in verse 9, the teaching here is the teaching concerning the deity of Christ especially regarding His incarnation by divine conception.

Therefore, it is incumbent upon every believer to examine oneself regularly so as to ascertain one's position in God. 1 Corinthians 13:5 *"Examine yourself whether ye be in the faith, prove your own. Know yet not yourselves, how that Christ is in you, except you are reprobates (or cast away)".* In the current 21st century Church, a lot of changes are happening. God's archenemy Satan knows, His time is up therefore He has to achieve speedily his agenda of derailing, dislocating, distorting the purpose of Christ on the earth. He knows and we also as believers should know that the end is near. The devil is desperately working with urgency. He has become so sophisticated, incisive, aggressive, strategic and more daring in His approach. Therefore, as believers we need to be firm on the truth, Jesus Christ. Mathew 24:24, *"For there shall arise false Christ's and false prophets and shall shear grens and wonders in so much that if it were possible they shall deceive very elect".*

The church needs to refocus on the basic teachings of Jesus Christ and His Kingdom. We do not pursue miracles, or signs and wonders but Christ and His Kingdom Hosea 6:2, *"Then shall we know if we pursue on to know the Lord ...."* Luke 12:32, *"..... the Father's good pleasure is to give you the Kingdom".* The Bible says Mark 16:17 *"..... And these signs shall follow them that believe in my name ......"* It is an unfortunate development noticeable in the present day Church that some among the saints are so obsessed with miracles and the spirtual spectacular and in the process missing Christ. Certain writer called this group of believers in the church **_miracle-manics and prophesy-manics_**, some of these believers basically lack the foundational doctrine of Christ. The goal of a believer should be Christ and His Kingdom. Miracles are the by-product of the believer's pursuit of Christ. Those who hunger and thirst for Christ (Matthew 5:6). Colossians 1:23 ...... *"continue in the faith grounded and rooted and be not moved away from the hope of gospel ....."* (Matthew 7:24-27). Our foundation should be Christ the rock.

The prophet (Isaiah 61:3) speaks of the **"planting of the Lord".** We need to be the fruit of righteousness. We should not be deceived by the glamour and the spectacular at the expense of the gospel of Christ.

2 Timothy 2:19, *"The Lord knows them that are his ...."* (Ephesians 4:14). We need to deepen ourselves in His word to counter deception. Man because of the body of flesh which is yet to be redeemed is more susceptible to satanic deception than to the Spirit of God. The tendency to gravitate towards the carnal mind and the sinful nature is extremely high. God has spoken and is still speaking to the church, Revelation 3:6 *"He that has an ear let him hear what the Spirit is saying to the churches".* There is an urgent and desperate need for a reconfiguration and renewal of our minds to realign with the word of God. Be ready the last trumpet is about to sound. Do

not hold on the perishable and earthly things for all shall pass away but His word shall remain, Mathew 24:35 *"Heaven and earth shall pass away but my words shall not pass away".* We need to disengage ourselves from all the voices and excesses prevalent in the church today. There is an insidious infiltration of the replacement theology in the church. This Theology has its roots from the Babylonian culture whose founder and ancestor is Nimrod (Genesis 10). This is a humanistic philosophy which gives pre-eminence to man and is the source of rebellion and idolatry. Many have shipwrecked in the faith (1 Timothy 1:19).

Anti-Christ Philosophies

The controversy in the world today is not about the existence of a universal God, the Creator, but the methodological processes of worshipping Him. Christ is the epicentre of all socio- religious conflicts in the world today. Many believe that there is a God, a metaphysical or transcendental power which is in control of the universe. However, not many believe in the mediatory role of Christ as clearly articulated in scriptures, 1Timothy 2:5, *"For there is one God, and one mediator between God and men, the man Christ Jesus."* For us who are of the Christian faith believe that Jesus Christ is Lord and Saviour of mankind and the only mediator between God and man. As Jesus said in John 14:6, *"I am the way...... unto the Father...."* 1Timothy 4:10, *".......who is the Saviour of all men."*

Basically, the religious ideological philosophy of anti-Christ is to deny the personhood or manhood of Christ They blatantly deny the biblical reality that Jesus was manifested in the flesh as documented in the scriptures. In the Bible the Greek prefix anti-, has two main meanings. First it means against, and the second meaning is, in place of or instead of. This indicates that an anti-Christ is against Christ and also replaces Christ with something else. Satan, over generations past has used the strategy to overthrow

Christ and His purpose by indoctrinating mankind with dogmas and philosophies which are either against or replacing Christ. Satan's war is not necessarily against God but His Christ. For in Christ all things consist (Colossians 1:17). Ephesians 1:23, *"... which is his body, the fullness of him that filleth all in all."* Christ is the essence and universality of who God is.

Brethren, we are living in the last days of the closing of an age. We have to be constantly in tune with the voice of the Lord so that we may not be led astray. Satan is indefatigable and is determined to complete his destructive assignment that is to kill, steal and destroy (John 10:10). We have to stay focused on the word of God and submit ourselves to the splendid and transformative guidance of the Holy Spirit.

Some various philosophies to guard against

Materialism

As a summary, we need to apply the word correctly and apply wisdom when approaching issues concerning money and its management in the church. A balanced approach guided by the scriptures is needed when dealing with monetary and financial issues. Revelation 10:10, *"And I took the little book out of the Angel's hand, and ate it up, and it was in my mouth sweet as honey as soon as I had eaten it my belly was bitter."* Now we realise the need to correct these entrenched positions among believers, particularly ministers of the gospel, with regards to money, wealth and riches. This can be a bitter herb to chew as we know change is not always exciting in fact, metaphorically, genuine and real change can be as tough or hard to experience, it's like a man trying to break a back of an elephant with a sword.

Individualism

1 Corinthians 2:16, *"For who hath known the mind of the Lord, that he may instruct him? But we have the mind of Christ."* The expression the "mind of Christ" here means the perspective, view point or consideration which is Christ-centred. Individualism is a philosophy which has its roots in Satan. One is only persuaded to look for himself/herself without the considerations of others. Just as it is in the world so it has also noticeable in the church. The world believes in the "one man for himself and God for us all" philosophy. This is Satanic, egoistic, and humanistic dogma and does not find any respect in scriptures. Competition, strife and conflicts among believers emanate from this satanic dogma. Some church leaders even fight for pre-eminence and recognition with the objective of achieving celebrity status. God is not looking for celebrities. We need to have the Spirit of Christ which exudes humility, patience and servant-hood. Actually, Christ is the embodiment and epitome of, Galatians 5:22 *"But the fruit of the Spirit is love, joy, peace, longsuffering, gentleness, goodness, faith......"* We are supposed to operate and function as a body, expressing the attitude of Christ, Philippians 2:5-8. Ephesians 4:5, *"One Lord, one faith, one baptism."*

This Spirit of individualism is actually divisive and retrogressive. This was so pronounced at the church of Corinthians, (II Corinthians 10:12). We see the apostle rebuking believers who were busy comparing themselves among themselves. It is unfortunate this spirit does not exalt Christ but man. This is the spirit of Diotrephes.

3 John 1:9, *"I wrote unto the church but Diotrephes, who loveth to have the pre-eminence among them receive us not."* We see this manifested in the church today. This is where the "man of God" syndrome emanated from. The man of God becomes the centre of attention. All eyes should be on him and he becomes the centre of attraction and he is the undisputed and has unquestioneable spiritual "powers. The man of God behaves like he has the franchise of power and is always expected to perform to the satisfaction of his audience;

the congregants. The church becomes a theatre for performance rather than a place of genuine worship. The **man of God behaves like a, 'spiritual god father" invested upon him are esoteric and autocratic powers .** However, in perspective it is not necessarily wrong to use this term, Man of God, but should be in the context of respect and honour not to deify man. In any case this term is mainly pronounced in the Old Testament and only mentioned once in the New Testament when Apostle Paul is writing to the young pastor Timothy on a specific subject (2Timothy 3v17) . It's unfortunate however that among some believers in some churches this simple term " Man of God" has developed into a subtle manipulative doctrine. In the socio-religious context existing today this term now refers to the one close to God or used of God and possessing certain outstanding divine qualities enveloped in certain charismatic anointing. Regrettably, these are unacceptable excesses which we should guard against at all cost.

However, we should take note of the truth. We need to honour and respect those who minister, 1Timothy 5:17 *"Let the leaders that rule well be counted worthy of double honour, especially those who labour in the word and doctrine."* There is the need to avoid excesses and a balanced approach in the application of the word is always of necessity. Dr. Chaplan says, *"**Applicationality in the perspective of contextuality**",* implying that our application of the word should always take into account the contextual aspect to maintain balance. No extremes or eisegesis (reading into the text) in view of wanting the text to speak what you want. This has led many astray in failing to rightly divide the word. Also important to note is that when the scripture emphasises on rightly dividing the word so it implies that the word can be wrongly divided, that is, hermeneutically misinterpreted. We need the "sound doctrine" not listening to itching ear teachers.

2 Timothy 4:3, *"For the time will come when they will not endure* **sound doctrine***; but after their own lusts shall they heap to themselves teachers, having itchy ears."* God is speaking and has spoken.

Dr Patrick Nyamadzi (PhD)

Humanism

This is the deadliest of them all. This philosophy encourages man not to be dependent on God but on self. God does not want us to be independent of Him. The Father cherishes the dependence of His people on Him. This is His pleasure. No matter how technologically advanced man can be; man needs God. This philosophy, HUMANISM, is worldly and sadly it has found its footing in the present day church. It has contributed to the desupernaturalisation, secularisation and apostatisation of the Holy Scriptures of the Bible. This worldly dogma advocates for man's self-supporting efforts in dealing with the affairs of this life. It has a flavour which is similar to the atheistic New Age Movement which claim that man by himself is a deity so there is no need of God. We should not be deceived there is no substitute to God (1 Corinthians 4:4 We should remember that in the Garden of Eden from Genesis this was the insidious and subtle inspiration of Satan which resulted in the tragic and treasonous fall of man.

Hedonism

This is purely a worldly philosophy but unfortunately it has invaded the church today. It has its roots from narcissism. It encourages the pursuit of worldly pleasure and sensual indulgence. As long as you feel good about it, be happy. This is essentially a fleshly-driven mindset which does not recognise the validity and authenticity of the Bible, *1John 2:6 "He that saith he abideth in him ought himself also so to walk, even as he walked."* We need to stay firm in the Word and remain focused so we can correctly represent Him on earth.

Only God's voice should be relevant.

We need to consider this matter of God's speaking. If there is a God in the universe, what would be the first thing that He would do? Certainly before anything, He would speak. If God is living, He must certainly speak. If He is real, His speaking testifies His reality. The entire church activity should be acting on what God is speaking. He is the speaking Father and His speaking demystifies his existence as God. Since eternity past, He has spoken a million times. His speaking is the origin of the Bible. In actuality, the Bible is a composition of the speaking God. He is speaking in your heart and in your spirit. **Christianity is the only faith which claims that the worshipped dwells in the worshipper.** What is God speaking? God's speaking is not only the word it is also His breathing when He speaks. He breathes Himself into us. Victory or defeat of a believer is depended on the ability to hear His voice. Isaiah 30:31, *"For through the voice of the Lord shall the Assyrian be destroyed."*

The voice of God which is the embodiment of His revelation makes the difference in this life. So every believer must endeavour tirelessly to hear His voice. Jesus said, *"My sheep hear my voice and I know them"* John 10:27, (Psalms 29:3-9). See in these scriptures there is emphasis on the "voice" of God. When Jesus took the disciples to the Mount of Transfiguration (Mathew 17:5) God Himself, commanded us as the body of believers to hear Him. Jesus His Son *"............. **Hear ye him"*** The living God imparts Himself into us by speaking. He wants to transfuse Himself into use. This is mainly accomplished by speaking. The more He speaks the more His divine elements will be imparted or transfused into your being and produces light. With this light, there is understanding, vision, wisdom, and knowledge. Light produce the ability to see things in their correct perspectives.

There are some people who have other peculiar theological and religious persuasions. They do not believe that God speaks to his people. In this book, we are not trying to emphasize Christian epistemology. We believe in the gifts of the Spirit, particularly the gift of prophecy. But we strongly believe all gifts should operate with the confines of biblicity. The prophetic phenomena witnessed today has to be interrogated with scriptural checks and balances to avoid the enemy's manipulation and subtlety. According to research a number of believers have fallen to the influence of familiar spirits, spiritism and divination which has its roots in Satan. Apostle John articulately expressed this point in Rev 2:13-14, *"I know thy works, and where thou dwellest, even where Satan's seat is: fast my name, and hast not denied my faith, even in those days wherein Antipas was my faithfully martyr, who was slain among you, where Satan Dwelleth. But I have a few things against thee, because thou hast there them that hold the doctrine of Balaam, who taught Balac to cast a stumbling block before the children of Israel, to eat things sacrificed unto idols, and to commit fornication."*

To avoid these possible demonic influences the teaching ministry of word should gain pre-eminence. Spirits have to be tested by the Word. 1 Thessalonians 5:19-21, *"Quench not the Spirit. Despise not prophesying. Prove all things; hold fast that which is good. "The word clearly give us the much needed spiritual balance so as to maintain that important prophetic biblical operational uprightness.*

Different Ideological Persuasions

We are witnessing a generation which has embraced multi-culturalism, polytheism, relativism, modernism and post-modernism which to a certain extent are influenced by the inevitable sociological phenomenon of globalisation. There is cultural cross-pollination which has resulted in acculturation, *which is, the assimilation of different cultures* .and this has largely created noticeable distortions in the way humanity view the true God "Elohim" our Creator. The polytheists, those who believe in many gods have spread their influence all over, more predominantly in the Asian countries like in India and Pakistan etc. There we find man some so primitive they see gods everywhere and in everything. Their religion is animistic (believing in animals). They deify almost all objects around. We know from start to finish the Old Testament is a record of a conflict between God and the gods. Again and again, the primary and ascendency of the God of Israel is triumphantly proclaimed. To Him several times is given the title "God of gods", (Deuteronomy 10:17, Joshua 22:22, Psalms 136:2). But the gods are always in the background. This is the reason our God is speaking to his people for a clear distinction and demarcation to be drawn. However, Satan in his shrewdness and craftiness, has tried to counterfeit. But the Spirit of Christ is loudly speaking through and in man to bring clarity to humanity on who the true God is. (Habakkuk 2:14), 2 Corinthians 2:11, *": for we are not ignorant of his devices.* With the spiritual "technologies" (spiritual gifts) given to us when he ascended we have the spiritual capacity as believers to counter Satan's agenda and all his nefarious strategies.

Mathew 16:18, *"And I say also unto thee, that thou art Peter, and upon this rock I will build my church; and the gates of hell shall not prevail against it."* Jesus was explaining to his disciples with the view to help them understand who He was. This scripture, over the years I heard it preached and applied differently. To some, the rock is Peter's revelation of Christ which the church was to be built on. Others say the rock was Peter himself as a person on him the church of Jesus Christ was to be built. Another school of thought is that it is the doctrine of Christ. All these interpretations could be correct but contextuality may be a challenge in embracing all of them.

An analysis of Mathew 16:18 demands that the historical context has to be given its due consideration. During the time of Jesus Christ polytheism and pantheism was prevalent. All forms of idolatrous monumental sculptures typified the methodology of worship. Historically and archaeologically, tradition has it that the rock Jesus referred to was a real physical rock. Geologically, many rocks were scattered in that vicinity. These rocks or rock were used by pagans or heathenistic deities as places of worship. They would carve the rocks as sculptors do and then form geological structures useable as altars of their gods for various religious sacrifices. Actually, Jesus physically pointed to the rock and said upon these rocks He was to build His Kingdom. In light of this analysis, I would like to draw your close attention to **the principle or paradigm of superimposition** This principle essentially gives us an interesting socio-religious and political perspective on the balance of power in kingdom dynamics. The stronger kingdom in influence and power overlies and overshadows the lesser kingdom to its physical or spiritual extinction. The stronger kingdom or power, in this context, Christ, the universal God incarnate, becomes the **superstructure** on the diffused lesser structure as total show of supremacy and power. On this scripture we see clearly the ideological indoctrination of His disciples. At this stage, this was necessary as part of the preparation for the grand finale the Cross and the establishment of the Church after Pentecost. He needed to instil in them a fighting and conquering spirit. Actually, from this scripture we see the pronouncements and declarations by Christ as a show of strength and power. Prophetically, Matthew 16 :18 is like a compressed summation of the eschatology persistently articulated in the book Daniel and Revelation. The use of the **term build** brings us to the revelation of the New Jerusalem which is the ultimate focus of Christ and the Church' ……..*upon this rock I will build my Church………'Christ here is making a declaration as the ultimate Supreme Judge with the final authority. At law this is called the summary jurisdiction, the final authority in court to release a judgement.*

This scripture is profound in essence and its prophetic content than most preachers simplistically consider. Christ is implying that there is to be a distinct superimposition of kingdoms. All ant-Christ spirits, ideological philosophies, dogmas, socio -theological and political paradigms against His kingdom agenda were to be superimposed by His power. This was also the heralding of the fulfilment of Isaiah 9v6-7.......... **the government shall be upon his shoulder v7 Of the increase of his government............"** **and also Philippians 2 v10 ....every knee shall bow ....** All other kingdoms set up by different gods or principalities referred to in Daniel 2:34-35, had to be subdued *"Thou sawest till that a stone was cut out without hands, which smote the image upon his feet that were of iron and clay, and brake them to pieces. Then was the iron, the clay, the brass, the silver, and the gold, broken to pieces together, and became like the chaff of the summer threshing floors; and the wind carried them away,* ***that no place was found for them; and the stone that smote the image became a great mountain, and filled the whole earth"****,* Ephesians 2:6, *"And hath raised us up together, and made us sit together in heavenly places in Christ Jesus."* Colossians 2:15, *"And having spoiled principalities and powers, he made a shew of them openly, triumphing over them in it."* We have discovered that he has also made us kings and priests. Rev 1:6, *"And hath made us kings and priests unto God and his Father; to him be glory and dominion for ever and ever. Amen."* (Romans 5:17). We therefore have to reign in the life because of the abundance of grace provided to us by His redemptive accomplishments and exploits.

Reflections

On the matter of kingdom, we hear Apostle John the revelator alluding to the supremacy and transcendence of the kingdom of God over other kingdoms. (Revelation 11:15) Our God is supreme and reign above all other gods. Apostle Paul said in his own day, "gods many and lord many" but there is one God and one Kingdom. The kingdom of God is advancing and conquering. Like what Dr W C Frazer stated in his Thesis on, **The Anatomy of Kingdom Dynamics**, *the advancability, unconquerability and invincibility of Church of Jesus Christ.* We have a promise of victory in Christ the Lord and Saviour of mankind.

The kingdom of darkness cannot prevail and will not prevail against the church. The church is a triumphant entity empowered by the Spirit of resurrection. God in resurrection, ascension of Christ and the Spirit of Christ is dominant and forever conquering 1 John 5:4, *"For whatsoever is born of God overcometh the world: and this is the victory that overcometh the world, even our faith."* Isaiah says chapter 9:6, *"The government shall be upon His shoulder......"* There is eminent replacement of governments in the world. Even at as individual person's level. Man, is a spirit which intrinsically governs human behaviour. The inward parts which the bible teaches invariably constitutes that internal personal government which in essence is supposed to submit to Christ the Spirit. Christ is actually securing and fulfilling the eternal purpose of God in man, the resting place of God. Rev 21:3, *"Behold, the tabernacle of God is with men, and he will dwell with them, and they shall be his people, and God himself shall be with them, and be their God."*

Recently, my wife and I visited India on a business trip. Our business friend in New Dehli took us for a tour in the city. We went to what they call the City of Temple. We were disturbed by the level of idolatry. There are idols believed to be gods all over. They worship different gods in India. We saw a number of grotesque images in ancient shrines or crude fetishes in private dwellings. Countless objects designed to be gods. Numb and dumb they do not speak or hear. "Oh God have mercy!" I exclaimed. The sight is spiritually nauseating. Matthew 16:18 resonated in my spirit what Jesus said, *"Upon this rock I will build my church"* God through Christ will superimpose His kingdom upon these gods.

I virtually wept from within as I remembered the grace and love of God. I remembered that God is loving, merciful and long suffering he would not want any to perish but come to the knowledge of Christ. His mercy endures forever and He is the preserver and sustainer of life. A flow of reflective scriptures came to light about God, His Christ and His Creator-hood. I realised truly we came from His hand we remain in His hand. One day all these people will be saved to confirm the power of the cross, His resurrection and ascension as Lord and the Christ. A number of scriptures caught my attention Job 7:20, *"I have sinned; what shall I do unto thee, O thou preserver of men?"* Psalms 36:6, *"Thy righteousness is like the great mountains; thy judgments are a great deep: O LORD, thou preservest man and beast."* Psalms 22:28, *"For the kingdom is the LORD's: and he is the governor among the nations."* Psalms 66:7, *"He ruleth by his power for ever; his eyes behold the nations: let not the rebellious exalt themselves, Selah.* Daniel 4:17, *"....to the intent that the living may know that the most High ruleth in the kingdom of men, and giveth it to whomsoever he will, and setteth up over it the basest of men."*

Therefore to all believers, it is important and so critical to tune in to the voice of God. The frequency of the heavens is increasingly connectable for the church to march on fulfilling Mark 16:15, *"And he said unto them, Go ye into all the world, and preach the gospel to every creature"*. We need to preach the gospel of Christ more aggressively than ever before. The heavenly signals are heralding the end of an age. The one found suitable to open the seal is on the throne. His mandate is to bring this age to its conclusion, Rev 5:1-5, *"And I saw in the right hand of him that sat on the throne a book written within and on the backside, sealed with seven seals. And I saw a strong angel proclaiming with a loud voice, who is worthy to open the book, and to lose the seals thereof? And no man in heaven, nor in earth, neither under the earth, was able to open the book, neither to look thereon. And I wept much, because no man was found worthy to open and to read the book, neither to look thereon. And one of the elders saith unto me, Weep not: behold, the Lion of the tribe of Judah, the Root of David, hath prevailed to open the book, and to lose the seven seals thereof.* This is the New Testament message of Christ, the Spirit, Matthew 17:5 **"...hear ye Him." The gates of hell cannot prevail against the new creation**.

Three

The Realities Between the Two Eternities

Rev 13:8, *"the Lamb slain from the foundation of the world"*. John 1:1, *"In the beginning was the Word, and the Word was with God and Word was God"*.

Genesis 1:1 *"In the beginning God created the heaven and the earth"*. Romans 8:28 *"And we know that all things work together for good to them that love God to them who are called according to his purpose"*

In Rev 13:8 we find out that the crucifixion of Jesus was an event planned by God in His wisdom before the earth was even formed. God in His omniscience knew that man was to fall so He eternally set in motion a redemptive plan for the restoration of man. To God, man through Jesus Christ is His irrevocable treasure. This is the mystery of His will, which is hidden through the ages (Ephesians 3:5, Colossians 1:26). The universe is a mystery. Why is there heaven and why does earth exist? Why are there so many millions of items in the universe? Awesome, an estimated 100000000000 galaxies and innumerable stars. Why is there man on earth? All these are mysteries. If God exist truly where exactly does he dwell? Is He somewhere on the corner of the universe waiting to dispatch orders to angels? Who created Satan and why? Where is the origin of sin? Can a detailed study of Haematology, a religious term for the study of the origin of sin, give us a sufficing answer to the question of sin?

All these are philosophical questions in the world of mystery. No any known astrophysical, geophysical, or anthropological scientific researcher can provide full detailed answers to all these intriguing questions. This can only be mystery hidden in the Creator and can only be known by revelation.

Redemption, how did the idea come? It is a mystery which have to be investigated from scriptures Rev13:8. It appears to us that all the events happening now in the universe in time are in actuality a replay of what has already happened in eternity past. It is like watching a delayed football match, the results are already known, "Whoa, whoa" what an awesome thought. This is probably the reason we have a justifiable reason to agree with a certain writer who said "Truly there is nothing new under the sun." From this thought we need to gain comfort even as we sometimes go through tough times and challenges in this life. The end is known by God. Isaiah 46:10, *"Declaring the end from the beginning..."* No matter what the enemy might try to do in frustrating the purpose of God, his end we know. He is fighting a losing battle he knows it, and we as believers should know it. Ephesians 1:19, *"And what is the exceeding greatness of his power to us-ward who believe, according to the working of his mighty power"*. This is the mystery of His will. Truly, we might not have answers to all questions but the word of God is able to shed light for a better understanding. Remember Deuteronomy 29:29, *"The secret things belong unto the LORD our God: but those things which are revealed belong unto us and to our children for ever, that we may do all the words of this law"*.

In reality, the accomplishments of redemption began with, Christ's incarnation and continued through His ascension. When he ascended to the heavens, redemption was fully accomplished. The coming of the Spirit on earth through the phenomenal Pentecost is referred to as Christ's descension, the unbundling of Himself to humanity and the regaining of man for God. Beginning at the time of His descension repentance and forgiveness were brought down to earth and poured upon God's chosen ones. This redemptive drama took place in eternity past and was only revealed as mystery of His will in time.

John 1 reveals the two section of eternity. John 1:1 refers to eternity in the past from the beginning. Verse 51 refers to eternity in the future when the Lord told Nathaniel that he would see the heavens opened and angles of God ascending and descending on the Son of Man. He was speaking of eternity in the future. Of course, we also must be conscious of the present realities of our eternal position as we are regenerated by the Spirit. If we put together these sections of eternity we have the whole eternity. Precisely, by definition and explanation, eternity is an integration of two eternities, the past and the present infused in the future. Essentially, eternity, like God the Creator is indescribable and inexplicable and it is not objective but it is a realm or domain. The bridge of time is in between these eternities. All the redemptive processes, incarnation, creation, crucifixion, resurrection, ascension, enthronement, exaltation and the descension of Christ as the Spirit took place in time after the cross at Calvary. This is the awesome wisdom of God in its highest form. In eternity past God planned and purposed but He did not do everything. In eternity future, God will not do everything, because at that time everything will have been accomplished. In eternity future we will simply enjoy His finished work in Christ. In eternity past he planned and in eternity future He will enjoy. What it translates to, is that man is just an expression of the finished product of redemption. His satisfaction and joy is to see Himself in Man.

In the study of our redemption in Christ we have come to the revelation in John 1:1. The language of the gospel of John is simple and brief but actually profound. Let us consider the first clause of the whole book of John. *"In the beginning was the Word".* Although the language is simple but the depths of the meaning cannot be fathomed. What is the beginning? When was the beginning? What a difficult philosophical question? Even in Christian epistemology and ethics we cannot find the definition or answer to this question. This is what makes the bible and our God a mystery. This is even beyond metaphysics. Another question in John 1:1 what was the word? However, I came to an understanding that the word, Word in John 1:1 from original Greek meaning is Logos, a genius and incomparable **idea**. So the word was the **"genius idea"**. God in His wisdom had a genius idea in eternity past. This idea brought in creation as it was in form of a word. Genesis 1:1, *"In the beginning God created the heaven and the earth"* and Genesis 1:3, *"And God said, Let there be light: and there was light"*. In verse 6, *"And God said, let there be a firmament in the midst of the waters, and let it divide the water from the waters"*, verse 9, *"And God said, let the waters under the heaven be gathered together unto one place, and let the dry land appear and it was so"*, verse 11, *"And God said, Let the earth bring forth grass, the herb yielding seed, and the fruit tree yielding fruit after his kind, whose seed is in itself, upon the earth: and it was so"*, verse 14, *"And God said, Let there be lights in the firmament of the heaven to divide the day from the night; and let them be for signs, and for seasons, and for days, and years:"*, verse 20, *"And God said, Let the waters bring forth abundantly the moving creature that hath life, and fowl that may fly above the earth in the open firmament of heaven"*, verse 24, *"And God said, Let the earth bring forth the living creature after his kind, cattle and creeping thing, and beast of the earth after his kind: and it was so"*. We then see in John 1:1 that the **idea** is declared as a reality, so we can safely argue and assert that John 1:1 can be interpreted in this manner. *"In the beginning was a genius idea, and the genius idea was with God (in eternity) and the genius idea was actually God Himself."* This genius idea became flesh and tabernacled (dwelt) among us in time though the idea was in eternity with God (John 1:14). This was the mystery hidden in God for ages and is now being revealed to the sons of God. This mystery is revealed in Christ in time, Ephesians 3:10, *"…..the multifarious wisdom of God manifested in time that even principalities and powers in the heavenly places cannot even understand but this has been revealed to the church"*. Christ is God's **idea** manifested in the flesh in time, 1Timothy 3:16, *"…the mystery of godliness: God was manifest in the flesh…"*

We have boldness, confidence and courage to stand against the wicked machinations of the devil. The wisdom of God prevails in every battle you encounter as a believer. Fundamentally, battles in life are won by the manifestation of God's wisdom. Miracles, deliverance, sign and wonders we need as divine interventions are contained in God's wisdom. Actually, behind every genuine miracle there is the instructive wisdom of God by His Spirit. We can confess boldly His word for we know what it contains. With this understanding, the finished work of Christ becomes a reality for life,

2 Corinthians 2:14, 1 John 5:14, 1 John 4:4, Isaiah 54:17, Romans 8:28, Romans 8:37, 1 Corinthians 15:57. All these scriptures and many others revealed in the bible become a reality for life.

As we fellowship with the word, revelation of Christ becomes a daily occurrence because God desires to manifest His glory to His creation. We begin to realise that the Word is the definition, explanation and expression of God. **Dr M K Maxidorrs, a renowned Theologian says, God through His WORD is the visibilisation of His Creatorhood** . God is mysterious but used His Word to express Himself to His creation, the Word which is His **idea** from eternity past. The emphasis here is on the philosophy of Christ, the **idea** of God. Conceptualise this thought. Therefore Christ as the **WORD logos defines, explains and expresses God.** Eventually, we realise that this word is God. God Himself is no longer, concealed and as mysterious. This revelation makes our God Supreme above all other acclaimed gods in the universe. This should strengthen our faith, authenticate and validate the reality of our God.

As sons of God we need to hold tenaciously on the revelation of the finished work of Christ. We can speak from the vantage position of the accomplished work of Christ with confidence, power and boldness. The objective legal fact stated in the Logos (idea of God) is now through revelation a subjective reality. Implying that what Christ did on the cross is translated into experiential reality. It is therefore important to fervently desire to pursue and apply the revelation of the finished work of Jesus Christ. This is our position as sons of God. In our daily walk with God, Christ is coming out of eternity to time to demonstrate the power of God to humanity. His transcendental attributes are expressed by His Spirit. Ecclesiastes 3:11, *"He has made everything beautiful in its time. He has also set eternity in the hearts of men, yet they cannot fathom what God has done from the beginning to the end (NIV)"*. Objectively man through redemption has become the vessel to contain God from eternity. This is the eternal purpose of God. It is unfortunate that the majority of believers in the Church life are ignorant of this truth. Regrettably, the devil has blinded many to this reality. Satan operates effectively where ignorance is more pronounced. Like what Dr Jimmycat reiterated in his Thesis on **'Spiritual Creativity'** *" the strength of Satan is derived from the psychological structures of ignorance which he build in peoples' lives and the systematic demolition of these structures bring deliverance.* "This is what Apostle Paul in 2Corithianian10v4 ....referred to as **.....strongholds**...

The devil's launching platform is ignorance. Apostle Paul in 2Corinthians 2:11 says, *"......for we are not ignorant of the devices"* (strategies, evil machinations, wicked schemes) of Satan. He is emphasising the importance of knowledge because knowledge brings enlightenment and illumination. Actually, in the bible ignorance is equated to darkness. Isaiah 60:2, *"....gross darkness the people....."* Mathew 4:15-16, *"The land of Zebulon, and the land of Naphtali, by the way of the sea, beyond Jordan, Galilee of the Gentiles; The people which sat in darkness saw great light; and to them which sat in the region and shadow of death light is sprung up"*. This was the manifestation of God in Christ as the Messiah to Israel as it was prophesied by the prophets. John 1:5, *"And the light shineth in darkness; and the darkness comprehended it not."* John 8:12, *"Then spake Jesus again unto them, saying, I am the light of the world: he that followeth me shall not walk in darkness, but shall have the light of life"*. Jesus emphatically declared Himself as the light bearer. John 1:7 and 9, John 9:5, John 12:35 and 46, Acts 13:47, Romans 13:12, 2Corinthians 4:6, Ephesians 5:8, I Thessalonians 5:5, 1 John 1:5 and 7, John 2:9, Revelation 21:23,

Revelation 22:5. All these scriptures and many more presented to us in the Bible highlight and emphasise the importance of walking in the light; and the understanding of this supreme revelation of the Word is the panacea for the menace of ignorance.

Prov11:9 says, *"Knowledge delivers"*. My conviction is that if one is saved and truly born again by the regeneration of the Spirit, he or she is actually translated from the kingdom of darkness to the kingdom of light, (Colossians 1:13). This is deliverance and the person becomes a new creation, a new species which the world has never known of. Then through the intake of the word that deliverance process is sealed to the frustration of demons. The demonic influence should not gain access to the spirit of the believer. Without cause, Proverbs 26:2, *"so the curse causeless shall not come."*

The dominance and pre-eminence of the word of God in the life of a believer renders the deliverance sessions sometimes practised in our churches unnecessary. It must be highlighted that deliverance is not a function of the flesh or human intellect, but the Spirit, Zechariah 4:6, *"...it is not by might, nor by power, but my Spirit saith the Lord of hosts."* The word of God becomes the anchor. The Word must take centre stage in your heart. If you are constantly harassed by demons and subdued by social life circumstances you need to check your attitude towards God's word like my mentor the late Professor Kambwete used to joke with us by always saying, "Check your wordiometer". The reading on your "wordiometer" determines your victory and success". This is true a genuine believer must have a word paradigm, *the WORD mindset.* It must therefore be emphasised that walking with God is not superstitiously magical and objectified. God is God He chose to define and manifest Himself through *His WORD* by the indwelling Christ the Spirit.

I cannot over emphasise the importance of the word. I am reminded of the story of the centurion in the book of Mathew 8:8, *"........but **speak the word** only and my servant shall be healed"*. Even Jesus Himself marvelled at the level of faith of this pagan. Therefore, for protection, healing and deliverance the WORD of

God should take the centre stage. There is therefore no need for *"spiritual improvisations" that is, any extra-biblical human efforts which might lead into spiritism or spiritual gullibility*, His Word suffices.

Sadly, thousands upon thousands have been deceived Deception is so subtle because it is actually the nature of satan Jeremiah 9v6 God warns '…..…*Thine habitation is in the midst of deceit, through deceit they refuse to know me"*…

No substitute is required. It is either Christ or nothing. Christ is the epicentre and the sum total of everything in God the Father.

If you understand the power of word in light of the finished work of Christ you do not need any gimmicks and spiritual drama to attain deliverance and the much needed freedom in Christ, the centurion said only "**speak the word**". Therefore, child of God, we have to be conditioned to follow the principles set by GOD in HIS WORD. Fundamentally, the Word of God is expected to be our culture. Am reminded of the great Samson of the old (Judges 15 :15) He slew a thousand men with a jaw of an ass. Did you know that the strongest part of human upper body is the jaw bone. The jaw bones upholds speech. Words are structured through the jaw bone. As a believer you are as strong as the words that come out of your mouth. Words are powerful, they can shape destiny. Prov 18 v21

Brethren, there is power in the Word of God. Luke 5:5, *"….Simon Peter said to Jesus, "Master nevertheless at your word I will let down my net"*. The bible later reported that they caught a multitude of fish such that their nets could not handle. Just following a simple instruction. ***His Word, His Word, His Word.*** At Cana of Galilee John 2; Jesus said, *"fill up your water pots"*. I say to you my brother or sister fill up your waterpots an overflow is coming your way if you can only believe His word, *"Only believe"* Mathew 9:28. I am amazed by the historical narrative on Abraham, the Father of our faith as stated in the bible. The bible tells us in Romans 4:2, *"he believed God…."* From a pagan background of idol worship, he just believed.

So we must believe that our God is able, (John 6:29, Ephesians 3:20 and 2Chronicles 20:20*). Only believe God*.

Only believe, only believe, only believe in the Lordship of Christ and *it is well*. Remember the Shunammite woman in 2 Kings 4, who against all odds proclaimed, "It is well!" Christ is the ultimate authority. Also an interesting analytical view of Abraham's walk with God. Romans 4:20 says *".....He staggered not ...."* This appears contradictory to scriptures because we know that Abraham took Hagar for wife; actually he had an extra-marital affair which God allowed but was displeased with. But because of his faith God justified him. The word **"stagger"** here in the original manuscript is disconnect. So he did not disconnect himself from the promise of God through unbelief despite the challenges surrounding his marital life. The important point here is for us to remain focused on the promise of the Word. Do not be disconnected from the promise. No backtracking. (Hebrew 10:38-39) Isaiah 55v:11, *".....my word shall prosper in the whereto I sent it ....."* His word will not return to Him without accomplishing, what he sent it for. (Jeremiah 1:5). We operationalize, and activate His Word by speaking and believing. This is the word of faith. Romans 10:6-8, *"But what saith it? The word is nigh thee, even in thy mouth, and in thy heart: that is, the word of faith, which we preach"*.

Jesus said in John 6:63, *"It is the Spirit that quickeneth; the flesh profiteth nothing: the words that I speak unto you, they are spirit, and they are life"*. The word has the inherent capacity to change any situation. Almost every great truth imparted to the church has been carried to the extremes by those who first received it. As a result the rest of church embraced the opposite extreme in overreaction. In biblical hermeneutics saints are encouraged not to form a doctrine out of one isolated scripture. We have to rightly divide the Word of truth in order to maintain the much needed balance in the Body of Christ. Deception is so subtle and insidious but lethal too.

We encourage people to remain in the Word and avoid any form of religious excesses or compromise. As some practises have ravaged the church.and the effects are noticeable in the form of deadly divisions, apostasy, confusion, witchcraft, and in some instances spiritism. Many are being swayed away. If we are led by the Spirit, as all true sons of God are (Romans 8:14) then He will faithfully lead us into all truth and victory in Christ. Always remember there is power in consistency and focus. Remember the law of focus and consistency.

We must always judge the root of a work before we devote ourselves to it, regardless of how "scriptural" it may seem. The Lord never said that you would know men or their works by how scriptural they are. It is possible to be scriptural and yet in opposite to a truthful position. The reality of a thing is known by the fruit it manifests. Is it the fruit from the tree of life or the tree of knowledge? It does not matter how much good a work seems to accomplish; the tree of knowledge is rooted, just as much in good as it is in evil. If the fruit is not Jesus, it is not life. We are often distracted from the river of life by little tributaries.

Jesus is sum total of all spiritual truth. All things are summed up in Jesus. Ephesians 1:10, *"That in the dispensation of the fullness of times he might gather together in one all things in Christ, both which are in heaven, and which are on earth; even in him"*. When we lose our focus upon this ultimate purpose of God; that all things will be summed up in His Son we then become distracted by lesser purposes of God which we then carry to extremes. Walking in the truth is not only understanding everything accurately but it is abiding in Him who is the truth. Growing spiritually is not just growing in knowledge but "growing up into Him", (Ephesians 4:15) and also growing in faith. Deception is not just misunderstanding a doctrine, it is actually not being in His will. The body of Christ is not made of many warring fragments, it is a living, functioning organism made up of many different parts that together make a whole. The true Body of Christ is not and never was divided. *"Since there is one bread, we who are many are one Body, for we all partake of the one bread"* (I Corinthians 10)

Actually, we are always admonished in scriptures against spirit of Balaam in his strategy to overthrow the covenant of God, (Numbers 23), but the voice of God triumphantly protected the children of Israel. Apostle Jude also highlighted the same admonition in his small writings on verse 11. Take heed, there are those designed to subvert the covenant of grace in Christ.

The time has come for the authentic person of Jesus be manifested in the nations. Zechariah 13:1, *"In that day there shall be a fountain opened to the house of David and to the inhabitants of Jerusalem for sin and for uncleanliness."* God is revealing Himself to the church by His Spirit the time has come to embrace the realities of Christ the Spirit, **Our ASCENDED and ENTHRONED REDEEMER**

Four

An Overview of the Crucifixion

Luke 9:23, *"And he said to* them *all, If any* man *will come after me, let him deny himself, and take up his Cross daily, and follow me."*

Luke 23:33, *"And when they were come to the place, which is called Calvary, there they crucified him, and the malefactors, one on the right hand, and the other on the left."*

1 Peter 1:10, *"Of which salvation the prophets have enquired and searched diligently, who prophesied of the grace that should* come *unto you:"*

The Bible is a book of doctrine and life. One of the most intriguing doctrines in the Bible is doctrine of the Cross, the Crucifixion of Jesus. No philosopher, historian or biblical scholar has managed to fully explain the wisdom of God with regard to the Cross. It remains the most controversial, mind-blogging and widely debated issue in human history. To the Christian faith the Cross is pivotal and central doctrinally. The distinction between the Christian faith and other world religions (faiths) is the man Jesus, him crucified. Universally, the controversy has never been on God as object of worship but the methodological processes of worship.

We believe God set a signature to the universe as an illiterate man signs his name with a cross. Rev 13:8, the crucifixion of Christ was not a private affair conducted clandestinely in an obscure corner of the peripheral province of the Roman Empire. It spans all space and transcends time. Before it was an act in history, it was a fact in eternity. We see in time God incarnate in Christ crucified by His creation. Mankind charged God with the introduction of evil in the universe but to God it was the phenomenal manifestation of His wisdom to the fulfilment of the spoken prophetic word over generations. No one of His word will go to the ground unfulfilled. Matthew 24:35, *"......my words shall never pass away"*.

The Historical Narrative of the Cross

The historical narrative of the crucifixion is that it was a diabolical way of administering death penalty which was an invention of the Roman Empire political establishment. It was an excruciating, humiliating, horrific and brutal way of punishing criminals of the Empire at that time. Particularly, those suspected or accused of intending to rebel or overthrow the existing political authority. This wicked act was applied on Jesus, the God of Creation. God planned it to manifest His glory and wisdom to His creation.

The historical narrative of the Cross is that the criminal or offender would be nailed on the Cross and remains there until decomposition. Of which vultures would then eat the decomposed flesh. Not getting much into a detailed explanation of the processes of the crucifixion itself it suffices to indicate that this was indeed a horrendous and inhuman, practise. But God in His wisdom ordained this to happen to His Son Jesus. (Luke 23:32 -33.)

What is the Spiritual significance of the Cross? It is not just a documented archaeological history for theological studies. The cross, essentially, is a very special part of the unique history in the redemption of mankind. Dr P K Sowell a renowned historian in Biblical Anthropology says', ***the Cross of Jesus is the Gateway to human Salvation'***. It is not meant to "botanize" the grave of the dead in a graveyard. But it is a symbol for the supremacy and wisdom of the Creator. Even the principalities and Satan himself cannot comprehend the wisdom behind the cross. Demons and evil forces only tremble at this Cross but they do not understand the all-inclusive power invested in it. Both the New Testament and Old Testament are replete of supporting scriptures on the historicity and authenticity of the Cross in relation to redemption. 2 Corinthians 4: 10-18, *"Putting to death of Jesus" His death resulted in the shedding of His blood. Without the shedding of the blood there is no remission of sin (Heb 9 v22.)*.......... The history of redemption cannot be complete without incorporating the birth of Jesus. The incarnation of Jesus remain an intricate and mystical piece of human history which historical philosophers and even the medical fraternity in the discipline of **Gynaecology or Obstetrics** have failed to explain. The mystery is a virgin conceiving without the normal human sexual reproductive act. Divinity infused itself into humanity. The humanly unthinkable was recorded. This was the essence of incarnation, God manifesting Himself in human flesh Isaiah 7 v14"**.......a virgin shall conceive and bear a son ...."This was the prophetic word fulfilled in a spectacular fashion.**

It has been interestingly pointed out that the Lord Jesus is the only person who ever lived before He was born. And is the only person also celebrated his death whilst still walking as a man on this earth. With joy, He looked forward to his death. This is not normal to an ordinary man. We see in Luke 12:50, Jesus indicated that he was constrained and desired to be released, *"I have a baptism to be baptised with and I am pressed until it is accomplished."* He was constrained and pressurised in his flesh to see his death. Therefore, He needed to die; to be baptised in the physical death; so that his unlimited and infinite divine being with his divine life might be released from within Him into His creation. John 12:24, *"Verily, verily, I say unto you, except a corn of wheat fall into the ground and die, it abideth alone: but if it dies, it bringeth forth much fruit."* This was a display of the amazing and awesome divine wisdom of God. One writer said, **"Eternity yearned to offload divinity on humanity"**. This is awesome piece of revelation.

The origin of Jesus still remains an enigma for generations to come. Professor Andrew Mob neatly notes, *"**He has no beginning,**"*

He was the beginning if there was beginning, if beginning is to be defined". He actually highlighted the pre-existence of Christ. Micah 5:2, John 8:23, John 8:58, John 17:5, John 17:24, 1 Corinthians 15:47, Philippians 2:6, 7, Colossians 1:15,

Hebrews 1: 1-3, Rev 4:11, Rev 13:8. These are scriptural verses, interesting to study as they give insights to the eternal origin of Jesus the Son of God who became the Messiah.

Christ's nativity was in another sense regeneration classically from "eternal generation". John 8:42, *"Jesus said unto them, If God were your Father, ye would love me:* **for I proceeded forth and came from God;** *neither came I of myself, but he sent me."* The historicity and Christology of Christ has been riddled with controversy particularly over the actual virgin birth, *parthenogenesis.* Dr S. K. Kimberly scholarly depicted it *"the birth of Jesus was the point at which eternity and time, the divine and the human, the heavenly and earthly intersected and converged".* Outwardly, Jesus was man but inwardly He was God. This is not simple theology but mystery personified.

The Death of Jesus

Concerning the death of Jesus to most people, the understanding is limited only to redemption. According to their concept, the death of Jesus was only for redemption. John 1:29, *"...behold the Lamb of God, which taketh away the sin of the world."* We believe this just as much as other Christians do, if not more. However, redemption is not just one aspect of Christ's death. Fundamentally, redemption is multifaceted, mult-dimensional and mult-layered, such that it will be unwise in biblical interpretation to consider one aspect of it. The doctrine of the cross forms a strong base for the spiritual capital needed by a believer. In 2 Corinthians 4, we see the aspect not of redemption and not of imparting life but destroying, consuming the outward man. For this reason, Paul says on 4:16 *"Our outward man is decaying"*. The Cross deals with old man in flesh. When Jesus was crucified the entire old creation, including all of us, were crucified. The Lord Jesus died for the fulfilment of God eternal purpose; not merely for the accomplishment of redemption but primarily as the first goal of God's eternal purpose is to terminate the old creation. Here, we hear the great Apostle Paul confirming the power of the cross with its inclusivity. Precisely, the necessity and efficacy of the cross is beyond human comprehension. Galatians 2:20, *"I am crucified with Christ: nevertheless I live; yet not I, but Christ liveth in me: and the life which I now live in the flesh I live by the faith of the Son of God, who loved me, and gave himself for me."* Essentially, in man, in us the flesh has to die in order for us to enjoy in full the redemptive rights through the cross. (Romans 8:3, Romans 7:76, Romans 6:6)

Jesus Christ is the fullness of God, (the *pleroma*) of God Himself. On the Cross he experienced a *kenosis* or self-empting. Philippians 2: 6-7, *"Who, being in the form of God, thought it not robbery to be equal with God: But made himself of no reputation, and took upon him the form of a servant, and was made in the likeness of men.* As believers we need to experience the transforming power of the Cross from within. No need for a believer to live a life riddled and compromised in sin, condemnation, defeat and frustration. The Cross is the climax of the love of God in manifestation. Love is unveiled on the Cross. All the attributes of God are displayed on the Cross. One theologian said, **It is hard to believe with the human intellect, that the compact existence of the universe can be influenced by a designed piece of wood.**

Professor Mayhem said", **the cross of Jesus is no longer a theological theory or hypothesis for academic discourses but an undebunkable and irrefutable fact of life for the existence of humanity".**

The intransigent Jewish religious leaders did not know that by crucifying Jesus they were actually terminating the priesthood which sacrificed bulls and goats in the temple. **It was the ascendency of a new priesthood**. When Jesus said, *"It is finished"*, their priesthood was finished, little did they know of the arrival of a new dispensation (*oikonomia*) Matthew 27:51-54, *"And, behold, the veil of the temple was rent in twain from the top to the bottom; and the earth did quake, and the rocks rent; And the graves were opened; and many bodies of the saints which slept arose, And came out of the graves after his resurrection, and went into the holy city, and appeared unto man. Now when the centurion, and they that were with him, watching Jesus, saw the earthquake, and those things that were done, they feared greatly, saying, Truly this was the Son of God."* In this text we see an amazing phenomenon. Bodies came out of the graves and and got to the city. This is intriguing. **Question**? In what form, structure and dressing these people had? Did these people go into the society and incorporated? Substantially it is inconceivable to visualise this episode. No one knows or knew what this meant. We can only speculate that this was probably a foreshadow of the resurrection which is to come towards the opening of the sixth seal in the closing of the age.

However, important also to note is that the Holy of the Holies in the physical temple was no longer the home of Jehovah. He had moved out of the physical Temple. Jesus had fulfilled the Abrahamic covenant and of the Mosaic law. There was no need for priesthood in the temple to do innumerable ritualistic sacrifices. There was no more the Holy of Holies, a place for the atonement blood to be sprinkled. When Jesus said, *"I will destroy this temple and restore it in three days"*, the disciples did not even understand. 1 Corinthians 3:16, *"Know ye not that ye are the temple of God, and that the Spirit of God dwelleth in you?"* The new creation is God's temple today. His death and substitution will make the former physical temple and its priesthood unnecessary. He was to be inaugurated as the High Priest after resurrection and ascension.

He had made one sacrifice for sins forever and He is to sit down at the right hand of the Majesty on High. Isaiah 53: 4-6, *"Surely he hath borne our griefs, and carried our sorrows: yet we did esteem him stricken, smitten of God, and afflicted. But he* was *wounded for our transgressions* he was *bruised for our iniquities: the chastisement of our peace* was *upon him; and with his stripes we are healed. All we like sheep have gone astray; we have turned everyone to his own way; and the LORD hath laid on him the iniquity of us all."*

Here is a picture of the substitutionary sacrifice of Christ in the ninth verse. Isaiah says, *"He made his grave with the wicked and the rich man in his death".* Actually, the word "death" is plural in Hebrew indicating that Jesus died twice on the Cross. He died spiritually the moment that God laid our sin upon Him. The moment that *"He who knew no sin became sin"* that precious body became mortal and could die physically. But now He is the God-forsaken Son of God hanging upon the Cross.

John 19:31-35, *"The Jews therefore, because it was the preparation, that the bodies should not remain upon the cross on the Sabbath day, (for that Sabbath day was an high day,) besought Pilate that their legs might be broken, and* that *they might be taken away. Then came the soldiers, and brake the legs of the first, and of the other which was crucified with him. But when they came to Jesus, and saw that he was dead already, they brake not his legs: But one of the soldiers with a spear pierced his side, and forthwith came there out blood and water. And he that saw* it *bare record, and his record is true: and he knoweth that he saith true, that ye might believe."* The piercing of the body of Jesus with a spear and the subsequent gushing out of water and blood was typifying the formation or creation of a new man just like God in the beginning of Genesis builded a woman from the rib side of Adam. We therefore see that redemption was not just a simple act but an eternal process wrapped in a prophetic word fulfilled in time, visible to the entire creation. Another writer called it*",.... **the choreographic and picturesque visibilisation of the Eternal mind of God"*** This was the fulfilment of prophecies spoken centuries ago on the sufferings and death of the Redeemer, in typology, the Lamb, Psalm 22, Isaiah 52,53. There are no fewer than twenty-nine Old Testament prophecies bearing on the betrayal, trial, death and burial of the Lord Jesus Christ, uttered by many different voices during centuries from the year BC 1000 to 500 BC which were literally fulfilled within twenty-four hours. At the time of the crucifixion, the precision in which these prophecies were fulfilled displays the splendour, glamour, majestic and supreme wisdom of our God. Many of the searchlights of biblical prophecy converge on the Cross and come to the brilliant focus on the crucified. None but God could have foreknown and foretold what was to transpire on that dark horrendous and wicked day on Golgotha.

Dr S. K. Bruss said, *"It was a colossal cosmic drama of redemption"*.

I am personally amazed by the power of the Cross and I desire to search more. One day I tumbled into a paper written by an old late Professor who was a Philosopher in Historical Metaphysics, before he died. He said, **"In my attempt to research on the credibility, authenticity and historicity of the Cross, one day I came face to face with the Cross and the truth that the crowned Lord** *of thirty trillion galaxies and constellations came down to earth to bleed and die for me and my sins. I was utterly broken down and could no longer theorize about it than I could bonatize on my mother's grave.* **It is a fact the Cross saves". "Whoa, Whoa, Whoa". What a testimony from a man who witnessed the power of the Cross. (1 Corinthians 15:3, Romans 5:8, Romans 14:9, John 10:18, Galatians 2:20). Dr Potek said,** *"We are saved by the Cross not by our attempt in the interpretation of it.*

'God forbid that I should glory" cried Paul, *"save in* the Cross of our Lord Jesus Christ"*. Galatians 6:14

One French writer speculated and said when Christ came into the world, there is one thing he asked for when he was walking about the city of Galilee and that was the Cross which to die. "When He was doing his carpentry work his imagination was only the Cross", he speculated, this is an interesting thought.

In Matthew 20:1-2, *"For the kingdom of heaven is like unto a man* that is *a householder, which went out early in the morning to hire labourers into his vineyard. And when he had agreed with the labourers for a penny a day, he sent them into his vineyard."* Immediately after giving the prophecy of the Kingdom, the Lord told his disciples that in two days the Passover was coming and that the Son of Man was being delivered to be crucified. The significance here is that, His crucifixion is the fulfilment of the Passover. The Passover was to be the last and it had been observed for more than fifteen centuries but now the Passover was to be terminated and in a sense replaced. By putting together the Passover and the crucifixion of the Son of Man, this was implying that His crucifixion was the fulfilment of the Passover and that He himself was the Passover Lamb. A type of Christ, 1 Corinthians 5:7. Christ is the Lamb of God, that God be Passover for us, the sinners as portrayed in typology by the Passover in Exodus 12. According to the type, the Passover Lamb had to be examined for its perfection during days preceding the day of Passover, (Exodus 12:3-6). Before crucifixion, Christ came to Jerusalem for the last time six days before the Passover, (John 12:1), and was examined by the religious leaders in a few days. (Matthew 27:23-22, 46), No blemish was found in Him and was qualified to be the Passover Lamb for us. The Son of God was then crucified. Satan and his demons celebrated, demons worshipped their gods. The evil men thought it was done. Little did demons know that it was the beginning of the end of their diabolical hold on the captured humanity. God in His wisdom had triumphantly overturned the tables. Eternity had offload GRACE on the entire human race. ***This is synopsis of His Crucifixion, THE MYSTERY OF AGES***

Five

The Mystery of the Veil in the Temple

From time immemorial God's history with man show us that God' in many times spoke in diverse manners to the prophets through types, shadows, numbers and symbols. In studying the Bible we call these typology, symbolism and numerology. In the book of Hosea Chapter 12 :10 the writer call these "........multiplied visions and similitudes............" In fact, the Bible with its original Hebrew and Greek language is a historically documented book of pictures. And symbols from eternal antiquity it is the only effective methodology God considered efficacious in communicating with His creation particularly Man.

An analytical study of these aspects stimulate excitement in our theological journey as is more revealing. Because man's finite mind cannot or could not comprehend the wisdom of God. We see most of these types and symbols and shadows mostly in the Old Testament and all of them have one objective or purpose, that is, to reveal Christ as, the Son of God and ultimately manifest His GLORY.

The Tabernacle of Moses was a type of both Jesus and the Church as both were the habitation of God. In Moses' Tabernacle, the closer one came to the presence of the Lord, the more sanctified he was required to be. When the Tabernacle of Moses was constructed and then sanctified for use, an unsanctified man could not enter to Holy Place or even look at the furniture. The penalty for this was death, (Numbers 4:20). This was to testify of the requirement of sanctification before we can see most of the Holy things.

When we enter the Tabernacle we come into the compartment called the Holy Place. The furniture here was made of "acacia wood" but it was covered in pure gold. This acacia wood was also the same material used for building the outer court of the Tabernacle. It was hard and twisted wood representing the fallen human nature. Always when the priest in entering the outer court.it was illuminated by the "natural" light of the sun. But in the Holy Place the olive oil burned in the lampstand (candlestick) typifying the Holy Spirit. In the Holy Place there is no natural light and we cannot function there with our natural mind but dependent on the Spirit. In the Holy of Holies the innermost compartment where the Lord himself dwells, the Mercy seat is gold inside and out. The light provided in the Holy of Holies is the very presence of God. We see by this the closer one gets to the glory the more gold there is typifying that we are changed into the divine nature by the glory. (2 Corinthians 3:18). As we get closer, the light by which we walk changes from natural light to the anointing of the Holy Spirit to the very presence and glory of the Lord.

Matthew 26:51-56 reveal the effect of Christ crucifixion. Verse 51 says *"And behold the veil of the temple was torn into two from the top to bottom"*, signifying that the separation between God and man was abolished because the flesh signified by the veil of sin taken by Christ (Romans 8:3) has been crucified. Hebrews 10:20

This was absolutely a supernatural phenomenon because the veil by virtue of its construct, it was a heavily built structure, approximately 500 meters by 300 meters using modern conventional measurements. The material used, according to the Bible scholars, was so heavy such that three hundred serving men (priests) were required to open the veil for the High Priest to enter the Holy of Holies. But the renting of the veil happened in few minutes from top (above) to bottom (man). Now this opened the way for humanity to enter the presence of God. What a wonderful effect of the Lord's death. His death was not martyrdom, it was an act of redemption and it all happened by the sovereign will of God in fulfilment of prophecies. **Essentially, His death destroyed death.**

Jesus was forced into the hands of the Priesthood and of the hands of the Roman Gentiles. These hands met on the sacrificed that they offered upon the altar of the Cross. Just as no offering was acceptable unless hands had been laid on its head under the Abrahamic covenant, the offering of Christ was made acceptable because the priesthood and the Roman government laid their hands upon our beloved Lord, *"The Lamb of God who was to take away the sin of the world."* This heralded the establishment of the new covenant and the beginning of the new creation; the circumcision of the heart. Colossians 2:11-12, *"In whom also ye are circumcised with the circumcision made without hands, in putting off the body of the sins of the flesh by the circumcision of Christ: Buried with him in baptism, wherein also ye are risen with* him *through the faith of the operation of God, who hath raised him from the dead."* And it was a beginning of a new priesthood. Hebrews 8:1-2, *"Now of the things which we have spoken* this is *the sum: We have such an high priest, who is set on the right hand of the throne of the Majesty in the heavens; A minister of the sanctuary, and of the true tabernacle, which the Lord pitched, and not man."* You should read carefully Hebrews 8:1-13. It tells us of the new covenant that is to be given to the new creation. It closes with this significant sentence, *"A new covenant, He had made the first old, but that which is becoming old and waxeth aged is nigh unto vanishing away."* There was an annulling of the foregoing commandment and foregoing covenant and foregoing priesthood and sacrifices. There was an inauguration of the new covenant as a new covenant people, (Hebrews 9:11-12, Hebrews 9:24, Romans 8:1-2). It is therefore important for believers to be always conscious of the realities of grace manifested in the New Testament, which is the new covenant, a new contract with different set of terms and references. Therefore, the importance of renting of the veil is experiential both at personal and corporate levels. Fundamentally, this phenomenon was a symbolic act to give believers access into the Holy of Holies, the place of intimacy with God. Experientially and symbolically you can hold on the horns of the altar through prayer. Revelations, insights and victories are realised in this realm, the realm of the Spirit. The good news to remember is that anyone who believes has access to the FATHER OUR CREATOR. It is no longer a preserve for a few selected individuals. **Glory to GOD in the HIGHEST the VEIL was rent, the universal accessibility became a reality. PRAISE BE TO HIS NAME FOREVER MORE.**

Six

The Reality of Resurrection

Matthew Henry, "the Shakespeare Commentators" made the point tellingly. ***"When Lazarus rose from the dead, he took his grave-clothes with him because he was going to need them again. But when Christ rose from the dead, He left his grave-clothes behind because he had finished with them forever".***

Professor Kimberly White, a renowned theological researcher said, ***'For Christ kenosis (self-emptying) was followed by pleroma (enjoyment of the fullness)".*** He came to the place of Skull, the very epitome of emptiness and became Head over all things filling the universe with His presence. The New Testament categorically assures *"He ascended up far above all heavens that he might fill all things"*, Ephesians 4:10.

This is perfect portrayal of our God in resurrection. The universal presence of Christ as experienced throughout the Christian faith is a unique religious phenomenon to all believers in the Christian faith. It produces a convincing proof in itself of the reality of the resurrection.

According to Bible scholars, resurrection is a miracle of reversal which belongs to the new creation. Old creation cannot comprehend this process. Dr Kelly Tom said ***"among the post-crucifixion phenomena, resurrection is an incontrovertible reality of all...."***

(1 Peter 1:25, John 11:25, Luke 24:34, Acts 17:31, John 14:19)

The historical narrative of resurrection is that it is an event which took place after the Cross – His Death. Jesus was actually raised from the dead. (Acts 2:24, Ephesians 2:20. Romans 8:11.) This was in fulfilment of the prophetic word spoken of Christ and was declared in His incarnate state. (John 12:24, Psalms 16:10)

The resurrection of Jesus was the greatest event that ever took place either in the sense realm or in the spirit realm. Satan is defeated. Death was permanently conquered. The Head of the new creation is a Victor. All members of the new creation are overcomers, masters of circumstances and of all demonic forces. He vanquished principalities and powers.

Rev 1:18, *"I am he that liveth, and was dead; and, behold, I am alive for evermore, Amen; and have the keys of hell and of death."* Colossians 2:15, "And *having spoiled principalities and powers, he made a shew of them openly, triumphing over them in it."*

Now He is about to take His own blood as the High Priest into the heavenly Holy of Holies to make the eternal redemption. Resurrection of the Lord let love loose. It enabled God to give eternal life a perfect redemption, a perfect freedom from Satan enslaved man. It made Jesus the Head of a new creation and it also made this new creation, man, a creative being who is in the class with God. A certain Bible Scholar said, **......resurrection had a sociological impact on humanity, by issuing a new social order which even anthropologists cannot academically articulate. The new creation was a new class of people in the society of God, hence, the (theo-class) the God class, a unique community of people.**

Out of that dark tomb came the light of the ages. When the Master arose from the tomb in Jerusalem, He gave to the world a new kind of love, a new kind of life out of which has grown new kind of ethics and a new standard of living that destroys all wickedness in the earth, living the old creation in the tomb.

It is amazing that the resurrection of Christ has influence universally. No one in history of the universe has ever exerted **posthumous influence** to the extent of our Lord and Saviour Jesus Christ. Since His death He has done infinitely more for humanity than any living person could possibly accomplish. His influence can be precisely described as *"effluence of affluence"* implying that influence is that property belonging to a person, mostly those in leadership positions, which flows into others, effluence (flows), affluence (wealth). So influence is the flow of those imparting qualities (affluence). No one has poured himself into the lives and hearts of people (men) as the Lord Jesus Christ. To billions His influence has most affluence as He became manifested in the flesh.

Historical Evidence (proofs) for Resurrection

1. ### Acts 1:3

The tomb was vacated. One presumably intelligent scholar asked me, ***"Would Christianity survive should a tomb containing Christ body be discovered?"*** I only said well you know what, without resurrection of Christ from the dead there is no Christian faith. But actually, that will not happen because it will be treacherous fabrication from detractors of our Christian faith. The authentic historical fact is that Jesus died and bodily rose again triumphantly on the third day. ***The emphasis on bodily has to be taken into account as some detractors preach that Jesus was only raised spiritually.***

2. ### The Grave Clothes

Another most important piece of evidence for the resurrection was the grave clothes. It was not only that the clothes were left in the tomb but the shape and position they had assumed at the entombment on the evening of Friday. The wind sheet had been wrapped around his body in the manner of the folds in material used of Egyptian mummy, sprinkled upon its cloth were spices, one hundred pounds weight. When Jesus rose, He passed through the shroud, without it being unwound. This was convincing to all observers that there was no way in which that could have happened without resurrection. Had the winding sheet unfold, torn apart or burst open from within, funeral spices would have scattered all over the floor of the grave. As it was, nothing was disturbed. The only observable change was the grave clothes, now unsupported by the body had fallen flat under the weight of embalming material. Indeed, He rose from the dead triumphantly.

We also note from the scriptures that resurrection was a process of transfiguration of Christ to be the life–giving Spirit. 1 Corinthians 15:45, "*And so it is written, the first man Adam was made a living soul; the last Adam was made a quickening Spirit.*" This is the all-inclusive Spirit who now enters the spirit of a believer. Now it is possible to talk of the new creation. When the Lord is in us the Spirit, the Son and the Father are all in us. The Triune God has habitation in a new temple not made with hands. This is definitely beyond the natural mind to comprehend.

More interesting was that the resurrection was also His propagation to produce the church as His reproduction. By His resurrection, Jesus our Saviour could be multiplied and therefore enlarged. Now you can consider Jesus' prophecy in John 12:24 The grain of wheat. Through His death and resurrection the Lord Jesus certainly has been multiplied and propagated. This propagation is for producing. His reproduction and the reproduction of Christ is the Church. Therefore, the Lord's resurrection is His propagation to produce the church as His reproduction. Ephesians 1:20-23, "*Which he wrought in Christ, when he raised him from the dead, and set* him *at his own right hand in the heavenly* places, *Far above all principality, and power, and might, and dominion, and every name that is named, not only in this world, but also in that which is to come: And hath put all* things *under his feet, and gave him* to be *the head over all* things *to the church, Which is his body, the fulness of him that filleth all in all.*"

This reproduction of the church, His body is to express Him as His fullness. This is ultimate issue of Christ's resurrection. This is the subjective aspect of Christ's resurrection as the life-giving Spirit. 1 Corinthians 15:45 *"The last Adam became the life-giving Spirit. The Spirit who gives life, the divine life must be the Spirit of God Himself."* John 20:22, *"And when He had said this, He breathed on them and said unto them, receive ye the Holy Ghost".* On Pentecost he manifested himself in full and He became universally accessible to all. (Acts 2:1-4). Resurrection had and has phenomenal creative capacity. If you just allow your sanctified imagination to kick in there, imagine the pandemonium in the grave yards when all the dead people resurrected. In what form where these people in? Did they have clothes and human consciousness? Did they run to their respective villages to start a new life? Could it be that they were also ascended into heaven as Jesus did? All these seemingly philosophical questions point us to one reality that resurrection is essentially God and is life. Amazingly beyond human comprehension and cognition. Therefore having gone through the theoretical historical and spiritual narratives on resurrection what is far more important is the contextual application at personal level. Resurrection is in reality a major foundational doctrine of the Christian faith.

May God give life to every seemingly dead situation in your life. May the resurrection power break every dysfunctionality, deprivation or infirmity in your life.

Seven

New Creation Realities

- ## The stick of Joseph and Judah

Ezekiel 37:16-17, "*Moreover, thou Son of man, take thee one stick, and write upon it, For Judah, and for the children of Israel his companions: then take another stick, and write upon it, For Joseph, the stick of Ephraim, and* for *all the house of Israel his companions: And join them one to another into one stick; and they shall become one in thine hand.*" Verse 19 "..............*Even with the stick of Judah and make them one stick and they shall be one in my hand*". Read Ephesians 2:11-19. We pay particular attention to verse 14 (NIV) says, "*For he himself is our peace who has made the two one and has destroyed barrier; the dividing wall of hostility*".

Here we have an inter-testamental reference of scriptures. We see the vision of the prophet Ezekiel a thousand years ago before Christ was crucified in time. In another perspective this was a precursor to the reality of redemption. Exegetically, (bringing out) we see a fascinating and an interesting picture of the mind of God with reference to redemption of the fallen humanity. God had an eternal plan in eternity past to redeem the entire fallen mankind. Such is the nature of our God. He is God of plan, purpose, objectivity and design. This is the reason our life as believers is not just a random visible web of unfolding events. In actuality, humanity is like a coin in His hand. Nothing just happens. This eternal plan had to be executed through a particular group of people. In His wisdom He chose a race through Abraham an idol worshipper in the heathenistic land of Ur of Chaldees. We see the symbolism here, the stick of Judah typifying Israel nation and the stick of Joseph in the hand of Ephraim typifying the entire Gentile nations.

The Great Apostle Paul a thousand years later after crucifixion and resurrection of Christ brings in this revelation (Ephesians 1:12-15) In verse *13* "*........we were far off are made nigh by the blood of Christ*". Verse 15 "*.......His purpose was to create in himself one new man out of two thus making peace*" *(NIV)*.

Apostle Paul is bringing the all-inclusiveness of the Cross of Jesus Christ. Now that He died and rose no one is expected to remain outside of the grace and love of God. It is like the Ark of Noah which was built as a refuge. As we might be aware of this typology relating to Christ, the ark typifies the Christ. No one is supposed to remain outside Christ. There is always new inisights when reading the Word of God. On Noah''s, ark, I always thought that Noah was safe inside the ark because he had built it according to God's specifications. I thought that perhaps it was the strength of the gopher wood and the soundness of the architecture that ensured that the waters of the flood would not come into the Ark. But I encountered a verse that shifted this whole paradigm. Let us read what Gen 7 :16 says ",......... *The animals going in were male and female of every living thing as God had commanded Noah* ....**AND THE LORD SHUT HIM IN**". Interesting, to note here is that even after Noah had built the Ark, it was God Himself who shut him in, in order to shut out the waters of the flood .....in other translation this verse says, ***The Lord sealed them inside***. It is not your good driving skills that keeps you in and shut devils, neither your good eating habits that keeps healthy, the truth is that, its **only God** through His Grace who can SHUT you in and shut out the devil that is seeking to devour you. He can keep you. This is the benefit and essence of the new creation paradigm. The entire creation needs the cover and security of this Christ. This is the glorious gospel of Jesus Christ. Titus 2:11, "*For the grace of God that bringeth salvation hath* *appeared to all men,"* Both the Gentiles and Jews have become one new creation, a new man with a distinct divine genealogical history linked to Christ. Ephesians 1:23 *".......who fill all in all and in Him all things, including nations consists."* **"For by Him were all things created, that are in heaven, and that are in the earth, visible and invisible .... (Colossians 1:16)."**

The one awesome truth of the gospel is that in Christ we are a new creation. We must therefore be conscious of the new creation realities in Christ. Galatians 6:15 says, *"For in Christ Jesus neither circumcision availeth anything, nor uncircumcision, but a new creation"* The **new creation is the mingling of God with man. The new** creation takes place when the Triune God in Christ through the Holy Spirit is to work into our being. This is the mingling of divinity and humanity. Living in this new creation reality is more beneficial to our faith than trying to keep the tedious and labourious Mosaic law. We have therefore to remain in Christ by faith. The mystery of this reality is that there is a divine union with Christ, Christ lives in us and we become a new creation A new class of people the God class. 2 Corinthians 5:17, *"Therefore if any man* be *in Christ,* he is *a new creature: old things are passed away; behold all things are become new."* Although we remain God's creation we are nevertheless mingled with the Creator. Having become one with the Creator, His life becomes our life, our living becomes His living. This mingling produces a new creation. This is entirely accomplished by faith in Christ. Living a life which is totally dependent on Christ the Spirit is the awesome reality and it also empowers us to function in the redemptive scheme of God's purpose.

John 15:1-8. Read focussing mainly on verse 7: *"If ye abide in me, and my words abide in you, ye shall ask what ye will, and it shall be done unto you."* We need to live lives which are fruit bearing in order to satisfy the Father. In the perspective of the dominion mandate given to man from Genesis, Genesis 1:26, 28. Here we see *"dominion" and fruitfulness* and is key in the fulfilment of the eternal purpose of God in man.

For the entire creation to appreciate God, man has to be the representative figure in the earth. In actuality, this is the original plan of God in the garden of Eden with first family, Adam and Eve before they fell to the manipulation and subtlety of Satan. Romans 8:19, *"For the earnest expectation of the creature waiteth for the manifestation of the sons of God."*. The visibility of the expression of God in man is the manifestation of His glory in the earth. Man in Christ is the epicentre of the economy, (administration, arrangement, dispensation) of God. Interestingly, we see the vision of the prophet Ezekiel in Chapter 1:16 *".......and their appearance and their work was as it were a wheel in the middle of a wheel"*. The entire universe is in a kind of a global revolution, in rotation. Man within the purpose of God, is the hub on the centre controlling the universal movement in the earth. This is the eternally agitating truth to the devil. The truth that man has authority and dominion like God and the capacity to express God unsettles and sets demons and their master to panic. This is the reason why Satan in his agenda always fight to dishonour God by corrupting man. Satan always want to assume supremacy over God. Yah, what a weird vision. Psalm 8:4-6, *"What is man, that thou art mindful of him? And the son of man, that thou visitest him? For thou hast made him a little lower than the angels, and hast crowned him with glory and honour. Thou madest him to have dominion over the works of thy hands; thou hast put all* things *under his feet:"*

Organic Union - What a Mystery!

The crucial point in our attempt to expound the philosophy of the new creation reality is the organic union with Christ which takes place spontaneously when we believe in Christ. Apart from the organic union with Christ, we cannot live to God. On the contrary we shall be alive to many things other than God. The concept of organic union is implied in Romans 7. In this chapter, Paul uses the illustration of married life. Marriage is a union of life. In this union the wife is one with the husband and the husband is one with the wife. In Romans 7:4, Paul speaks of our being married to Christ. "*So that, my brothers, you also have been made dead to the law through the body of Christ that you might marry another, even Him who has been raised from among the dead*". According to this verse, we have been married to the resurrected Christ. Between Him as the bridegroom and us as the bride, there is a wonderful union. We are one with Him in person, name, life and experience. This shows that our Christian life is a life of organic oneness with Christ. Therefore failure, sin consciousness, loss of identity, insecurity and fear should not be part of our walk with God. We are set free in Christ.

Romans 11, Paul added another dimension in his illustration on the grafting of a branch from one tree into another tree. In Romans 11:17-24..........**thou being a wild olive tree are graffed in among them and with partakes of the root and fatness of the olive tree.................v 24 ....for were cut of the olive tree which is wild by nature and were graffed contrary to nature into a good olive tree .... Paul** uses the illustration of branches from a wild olive tree being grafted into a cultivated olive tree. As a result of grafting, the branches from the wild olive tree and the cultivated tree, olive tree grew together organically. We as branches of the wild olive tree have been grafted into Christ the cultivated tree. Remember also Ezekiel's prophetic vision: The stick of Joseph in Ephraim's hand and the stick of Judah combined to become a nation. We need the understanding of the scriptures to have a proper perspective of our position as the new creation. Once we were wild olive trees, but now we have been grafted into Christ. This illustration indicates that the Christian life is not an exchanged life, the exchange of a lower life for a higher one but a grafted life. The grafting of the human life into the life of Christ. After the branch has been grafted into another tree, it no longer lives by itself. On the contrary, it lives by the tree into which it has been grafted.

Cutting and Joining

In the matter of grafting, there are two main aspects: the cutting and joining or uniting. Without the cutting there cannot be any grafting to talk of. If the branch from one tree is to be grafted into another tree, the branch must firstly be cut. After the cutting occurs, the joining or union takes place. The union is organic. The cutting corresponds to the death of Christ and the uniting to resurrection of Christ. In the death of Christ, our old life was cut off and in Christ's resurrection we were united to Him after further growth. The experience of the death of Christ causes us to die to the law whereas resurrection enables us to live to God. Hence to be dead to the law and alive to God implies the death and resurrection of Christ. Only by being grafted into Christ can we be one with Him in His death and resurrection. Practically, we are dead to the world, particularly to the religious world through the crucifixion of Christ. By the all inclusive death, cutting of Christ all inclusive death on the cross, we are dead to everything other than God. Because we have been grafted in Christ, when Christ died on the cross we died with Him. When he was crucified we were cut from the wild olive tree. This means that we were cut off from the self, the flesh, the world, religion and the law with its ordinances. Furthermore, because we have been grafted into Christ, His resurrection has also become our history. Therefore, we can strongly declare that with Christ we have been crucified, buried and resurrected. Galatians 2:20 becomes experientially a tangible reality.

It is, therefore, crucial that we see this vision, the vision of the organic union. This perspective should definitely change the way we live and see ourselves in Christ .The reality is that we are not just an ordinary *after thought creation of God* as the devil and his demons would persistently want Christians to believe. We are a peculiar people. We are royalty. I Peter 2v9,

We see that the enjoyment of the grace of God is altogether dependant on the crucifixion of Christ. The crucifixion of Christ indicates that all the requirements of law have been fulfilled by the death of Christ and through His death he has released His life that it may be imparted into us in His resurrection to free us from the bondage under the law.

In fact, the Cross is the centre of God's operation in His economy, just as Christ Himself is the centre of God's economy. Galatians 1:4, *"Who gave himself for our sins, that he might deliver us from this present evil world, according to the will of God and our Father:"* Although Christ was crucified for our sins, the goal of His crucifixion was to "rescue us out of the present evil age". Satan's cosmos, his world systems is the present evil age. As the devil, God's enemy, is involved with sins, so as Satan is involved with the evil age.

Furthermore, the Christ who lives in us is the Christ in resurrection. If Christ had not been crucified, how would He have been resurrected? This was to be impossible and if Christ were not in resurrection, He would not live in us. The Only Christ who can dwell in us is a resurrected Christ, a ***processed Christ, the Spirit,*** a Christ who passed through incarnation, human living, crucifixion and resurrection. The process through which Christ has passed affords Him the ground and way to enter into us as the Spirit and to live in us in His resurrection. The "raw" Christ, that is the objective Christ, the only begotten Son of God in eternity past would never would been life to us unless as processed Christ who can be the indwelling Spirit.

Practically, it is always important to bear this reality in mind that the Cross of Christ is both for redemption and justification. Through His death we have been redeemed from our sins and through death we have also obtained righteousness. **The ability to stand in the presence of God without the sense of guilty, condemnation and inferiority complex. He is our righteousness. We do not have to labour for righteousness but realise that it is the gift of God received by faith through Jesus Christ.** The teaching of self-effort as means to acquire righteousness is therefore

Dr Patrick Nyamadzi (PhD)

folly and humanistic. The devil uses this old-fashioned strategy to keep believers in bondage to his advantage.

(1 Corinthians 1:30, ...ye in Christ Jesus, who of God made unto us wisdom and righteousness.......... 2 Corinthians 5:21 For he made him to be sin for us who knew no sin that we might be the righteousness of God in Him".

Matthew 16:24, *"Then said Jesus unto his disciples, If any man will come after me, let him deny himself, and take up his cross, and follow me".* This has been a verse which has been interpreted in different ways in the church circles. Some interpret it to mean endurance through suffering. Some go to the extreme in stretching this scripture to mean the excessive suffering one goes through is equivalent to godliness or humility. In some instances, the forms of suffering believers experience is practically unjustifiable. Ignorance, poor decision making processes and the failure to apply the word of God in various situations and circumstances may contribute to these sufferings. Indeed, ignorance has its costs. However, of course, it cannot be denied that believers can go through persecutions which might results in suffering. It is always expected of the believer to find solutions in the prophetic word. I believe the carrying of the Cross doctrine has to do with the challenges one goes through in the course of fulfilling God's will. Obviously, by following or obeying God's will there has to be a prize to pay, no doubt about that. We have numerous biblical references to that, only that our space will not allow us to write all.

For example, the lives of the elders of faith mentioned in the book of Hebrews chapter 11; read all of it and then pay close attention to verse 37. And of course the lives of the prophets in the Old Testament and the Apostles of Christ and His Disciples in the New Testament. They suffered unbearingly to fulfil God's purpose in their lives. This is the reality of carrying the Cross of Christ which Jesus talked about in the book of Matthew chapter 16.

It is therefore clear that this "carry the Cross of Jesus theology" has sometimes been applied and interpreted out of context. The problem of this "carry your Cross theology" if it is not correctly interpreted can lead us to the humanistic self-help teaching which is always self-punishing. We need to wholly depend on God. Self crucifixion in the flesh is unscriptural. We need to have faith in the finished work of Christ and abide in the Spirit. The Holy Ghost is the game changer in the scheme of things as we live this life on earth. He reveals the deep things of God (1 Corinthians 2:11-14). God has promised in His word, *'I will never leave you nor forsake you"*, Hebrews 13:5. The life of a believer is entirely anchored on faith and the promise. No promise, no hope. He is a caring Father. Isaiah 49:14-15, *"But Zion said, The LORD hath forsaken me, and my Lord hath forgotten me. Can a woman forget her sucking child, that she should not have compassion on the son of her womb? yea, they may forget, yet will I not forget thee."*

With the full understanding of the revelation on the new creation realities, it is the expectation of God to see every believer in Christ to live a life of victory not defeat. Demonic influences should be repelled with minimum human effort. No need of the so-called deliverance sessions which sometimes exalts demons than our Christ. The subject of generational curses should not take centre-stage in the church. The Word should help us live independent of circumstances and always having in mind the sufficiency and the efficacy of God's word. Philippians 4:13, *"I can do all things through Christ which strengtheneth me."*

Acts 17:28 brings out another perspective of understanding our position in Christ. ***The "In Him" paradigm***. If we read in all the Epistles of Paul, we hear him over and over again reiterating this thought. ***In Him, In Him, In Him***. It is In Him we should abide. We should not lose our position as Satan lost in first estate as *the* scripture says in Jude 6, *"....the angels which kept not their first estate...."* These angels lost their position and became perverted and became dysfunctional to the purpose of God. May this not be our portion; we need to maintain our Kingdom focus and vision. Hebrews 12:2, *"Looking unto Jesus the author and finisher of our faith...."*

Every new creation is supposed to be a conqueror. The new creation has to dominate because he has its power from the unlimited divine source, the Spirit. Apostle John saw in his epistles 1 John 5:4-5, *"For whatsoever is born of God overcometh the world: and this is the victory that overcometh the world,* even *our faith. Who is he that overcometh the world, but he that believeth that Jesus is the Son of God?"* There is a concept of born of the Spirit to qualify to be an overcomer. We are born of God and we must appreciate our new genealogical reality. Our reconfigured and reconstituted identity in Christ. In implication, the believer has a new nativity. It is, therefore important for a believer to live with this awareness of the new creation doctrine. **Children of God are expected to know who they are in CHRIST. Glory to God in the HIGHEST.**

Eight

The Ascended Christ: His Ascension

The Ascension of Christ is one the biblical subjects not so often discussed in our present day Churches today probably because it is not a motivationally impressive concept or ignorance on the subject. Ascension is a phenomenon which is key to the understanding of the entire landscape of redemption. Most people consider ascension to be synonymous to resurrection yet these two are diametrically different especially on the application of biblical principles. Resurrection is, essentially, the coming back from a death situation to life or visibility. Definitionally, it is also the process or act of restoring to life. Yet, ascension is scientifically related to the principles of aerodynamics or aeronautics, which is connected to the study of the interaction between the air and solid bodies moving through it. Christ, therefore, pneumatically moved from His grave after resurrection and had to journey in the air, like our conventional aircraft engines, to the heavens in the glaring sight of Satan and his demons. (Col 2 v15)**........*he made a public shew of them openly, triumphing over them in it.*** This was an awesome reality demons could not do anything about. **This was an act of God by His Spirit**. The **victory theology** we shout about and believe in, is fundamentally underpinned on this universally impacting phenomenon which most of our present day teachers of the Word avoid or discuss in passing.

For a further explanation we can compare this phenomenon to the rising of Lazarus from the dead, John 11 .. Lazarus was raised but did not ascend. After his rising which was outstandingly spectacular he lived on earth for a while and dead later as a mere man yet our Lord, the Christ, ascended into the heavens of the heavens to be crowned the King of kings and the Lord of the universe Ephesians4v10".......*he ascended up far above all the heavens, that he might fill all in all things.*" This is an interesting perspective. In studying the dynamics of redemption it is important to note that the forgiveness of our sins was not complete on the cross, crucifixion because atonement had to be done by the presentation of His blood before the Father in the heavens which could only be achieved by His trumphatic ascension. From the principles of atonement we see in the book of Leviticus, we note that Christ was legally acting as the official High Priest which was typified by the Aaronic, priesthood in the Old Testament. Heb 9 v 14 " *How the blood of Christ, who through the Eternal Spirit offered himself without spot to God ...."This was in His ascension.*

I believe that Mosaic tabernacle spiritually gives the *dimensional paradigm or, the concept of dynamics of levels*, as there were dimensions to the tabernacle. The Lord had basic levels in His ministry to the multitude, the twelve and then the three. He spoke to the multitudes in parables and basics (outer court). To the twelve He revealed mysteries and they experienced the anointing (Holy place). The, three were privileged to see his glory on the Mount of Transfiguration, the Holy of Holies. A properly balanced church needs a ministry on all the levels as the Lord and the tabernacle exemplify.

We need to raise the standard in ourselves in our dealings with the Lord. We have to migrate from the foundational doctrines to maturity. I believe the saints need to get to the epicentre of interpretation of the Word which is typified by the Holy of Holies in the tabernacle and the three disciples meeting with the Lord of Glory at Mount of Transfiguration. We cannot afford to remain in the periphery of the things of God. Mediocrity and religious stereotype are a product of a lackadaisical and lukewarm approach towards the word of God. Most Christian believers are hijacked by Satan for lack of a strong foundation in the Word. A bigger part of the community of believers is swayed into spiritual delusion by strange doctrines. Ephesians 4:14, *"......carried about with every wind of doctrine...."* We cannot continue with the multitudes seeking bread and hearing the parables of the Lord only. The pursuit of the kingdom should be our goal to partake of His Glory. Sons do not always pursue miracles but Christ, the Spirit. We need to be Christ-focussed. This is the Spirit of son-ship. God, essentially, intimately connects to individuals not to a crowd, though His presence can be felt in a crowd therefore ideology of personalism is a fundamental component of the doctrine of Christ and His Kingdom.

In our study of the redemptive processes of Christ, we have discovered that redemption, through the Cross and resurrection cannot be full and complete without interrogating the aspect of the ascension of Christ. In essence crucifixion cannot be complete without the crowning of Christ as the King of kings as was prophesied by Daniel the prophet in Daniel 2:44, *"And in the days of these kings shall the God of heaven set up a kingdom, which shall never be destroyed: and the kingdom shall not be left to other people, but it shall break in pieces and consume all these kingdoms, and it shall stand forever."*

As life in resurrection, the Lord firstly appeared to His seeker. John 20:14-18. This was His first appearing after His resurrection. Mary, however, could only see Him, she could not touch Him because of the freshness of His resurrection was reserved for the Father. In His appearing to Mary, the Lord unfolded the revelation of the issue of His resurrection - the "brothers" and the "Father" (20:17). This is the revelation of the brotherhood and the Fatherhood. In His resurrection all His disciples have become His brothers and His Father has become their Father. Interesting to note is that on verse 15 it is recorded that Mary saw Jesus as a" gardener "giving us a picture of the first Adam in the garden of Eden. Little did she know the unfolding redemptive drama. The resurrected Jesus was the last

Adam with a mission to restore humanity to its original state before the treasonous fall of man.

As explained earlier, the ascension of Christ is the less, if not, least explained post-crucifixion phenomenon on the teachings dealing with the history of redemption. In John 20:17, the Lord said to Mary, ***"Do not touch me for I have not ascended to the Father".*** After he appeared in resurrection to His seekers, He secretly ascended to the Father on the day of resurrection. Most Christians do not see this matter of the Lord's secret ascension. Before the Lord ascended publicly in the sight of the disciples forty days later, (Acts 1:9-11), He ascended secretly early in the morning of the day of resurrection to the Father for the Father's enjoyment and satisfaction as He received the atonement to deal with question of sin once and for all.

In typology, the Lord offered Himself to the Father as "a sheaf of the first fruits of the harvest" and for the "wave offering." Leviticus 23:10-15. The firstfruit which was brought into the temple and offered in the presence of God as a wave offering typifying Christ coming into the presence of God for His satisfaction early on the morning of the day of His resurrection.

The Lord's secret ascension was the fulfilment of the word predicted in John 16:7, *"Nevertheless I tell you the truth; it is expedient for you that I go away: for if I go not away, the Comforter will not come unto you; but if I depart, I will send him unto you."* We see Christ ascended to the heavens with a resurrected body, and now in John 20, He comes back to the disciples also with a resurrected body. The Lord enters into the room where the disciples were with the doors shut (20:19). We need to unpack this phenomenon. We see the resurrected Christ entering a room whose doors where shut. This is intriguing and thought-provoking. Since the doors were shut, how could He enter with a body of bones and flesh? Our finite mind cannot comprehend this episode.

As recorded by Luke, Luke 24:37-40, the Lord showed His disciples his physical body and according to

1 Corinthians 15:44, His body was a resurrected body. Let me

make an illustration of a carnation seed. It has a tiny round body but when it has been planted and has grown out of the ground, it has a stem and a blossom. Is this not also a body? Before the carnation seed was sown into the ground, it had a little body. After growing out of the ground it had a different body. This is exactly what Paul mentions in 1 Corinthians 15:44, *"It is sown a soulish body, it is raised a spiritual body"*. This body is sown in one form and raised up from the ground in another form. The one sown is the original natural body and the one grown up is the resurrected body. After His resurrection, Christ had a resurrected body which was physical and could not be touched. Even though the doors were closed, Christ entered with His body. This is a mystery which searches for an independent theological inquiry. Dr Penny Drum (Phd) said," ***this was the height of metaphysics and trans cedentalism***' No human mind can fully comprehend this phenomenon.

In practical application, there is no situation, in this life which has no solution in Christ. No matter how complicated the challenging situation might be. Jesus is able to deliver. There is no demonic attack He cannot handle. The walls of Jericho were huge, historians actually say a 20tonne truck would drive on it, but the supernatural power of God destroyed this seemingly insurmountable wall. Read the story Joshua 6: by a single divine instruction. **What a miracle it was?** In fact tradition has it that the wall itself actually submerged into the earth. Our God is able if you can only believe. Actually, throughout scriptures God appears to be always dealing with not only difficult but the impossible. He is recorded as the God of impossibilities.

He is the God of turnaround who can suddenly appear at any given time to any situation. Dr. Mensa Otabel calls Him the God of **"Serendipity"**, the suddenly appearing God, and the God who manifest Himself to His people for His Glory. Only believe in His supernatural capacity to deliver. The ascended and the crowned Christ the Spirit is able to do exceedingly above all what we can ask, think or imagine. Ephesians 3 v20.

John 11:40, *"Believe and you will see His glory."* Our objective position as a spiritual reality is that we are raised with Him in glory, Ephesians 2:6, *"And hath raised us up together and made us sit together in the heavenly places in Christ Jesus".*

"Raised together", the spiritual meaning should then be that in His ascension we ascended with Him. We are with Him in His ascended and exalted position. This is the frustration demons have in trying to control a life of a believer. **Colossians 3:1, *"If ye then be risen with Christ ...."* verse 3, *"For ye are dead and your life is hid with Christ in God".* Verse 4, *"When Christ, who is our life, shall appear, then shall ye also appear with him in glory."*** He becomes the strong tower for security and protection. Fear not then child of God, the King of Glory shall appear. Psalm 24:7-10.

Christ in His Ascension

In the book of Revelation, Christ is revealed as the ascended one, (Revelation 5:3-6, 8-14). In the four gospels we see Christ the incarnate, living on earth, crucified and resurrected. However, we do not see much concerning Christ in His ascension. Even in the Epistles, we see just a little of the ascension of Christ. It is in the book of Revelation we see a much clearer portrait of Christ in the heavens after His ascension. The economy of God's administration is under Christ's jurisdiction and governmental authority. The entire universe is under His administration and supreme management. The part which we as Christian actually draw strength from is that realisation of the revelation of our position in Christ. We are co-heir and co-joint heirs with Christ. Essentially, because He effectively restored our dominion mandate we are in partnership for administering the universe. **This is the mind of God in the context of His eternal purpose.**

Nine

Descension of Christ the Spirit

Descension, the term is derived from the word descend meaning act of being drawn downwards from an elevated position. We see Christ as He is resurrected and ascended into the heavens He became the Spirit. In *order for Him to be transfused and imparted in man He had to offload Himself hence, descension on the day of Pentecost in the Upperroom. This is the Holy Ghost overshadowing humanity and the entire creation as it was from the beginning in Genesis.1 v2 ....*the Spirit of LORD moved upon the waters. At Pentecost the Spirit was now in the readiness to recreate mankind and reshape the entire creation as it was in the beginning". *"**The whole earth was filled with His Glory as waters covers the sea…(Hab 2v14)"***

We may say the conception of Jesus as our Saviour was His coming down not only from heaven but from God the Father. Likewise, His ascension was His going back not only to the heavens but also to the Father. The Lord's ascension was not the conclusion of assignment. Rather it was the initiation into the higher dimension of divine responsibility. Christ's ascension was His inauguration, His initiation, into His heavenly ministry. The four gospels talk of the Lord Jesus, the incarnate Christ, on earth. But in the book of Acts and the Epistles, articulates and reveal Christ is the wonderful person, all enthroned; exalted and glorified.

Christ's ascension was like 'sword' piercing eternity to initiate the universal fulfilment of the prophetic word spoken generations past by the prophets particularly Prophet Joel (Joel 2:28). The pouring out of His Spirit upon all flesh as fulfilment of one of the festivals, in Leviticus 23; *the feast of Pentecost*. This was a phenomenal display of the awesome wisdom of God to His creation. The timing, the accuracy and precision of the fulfilment of His prophetic word is interesting to note. He is, indeed, an awesome GOD the only wise GOD 1Timothy1v 17 Acts 1:8, *"But ye shall receive power, after that the Holy Ghost is come upon you: and ye shall be witnesses unto me both in Jerusalem, and in Judaea, and in Samaria, and unto the uttermost part of the earth"*. The disciples at this stage were occupied with traditional concepts; concerning Israel, Moses and keeping the law.

Briefly the Lord was telling them of the need to be transferred dispensationally. This **"dispensational transfer" or the transitioning** would bring in new theological paradigm concerning Christ, God and His Kingdom to all the apostles and other disciples. This was a milestone in revealing Christ in His totality. The Mosaic Laws, the Old Testament with its traditional concepts and practises had to be obliterated and considered obsolete. However, this is the reason we see time and time again the apostles even among themselves clashing doctrinally as a result of their involvement in the various Old Testament ritualistic practises and religious rites. For the saints in the Church life should therefore be conscious of the resurrected Christ and their position in Him. The Mosaic Laws are obsolete, tedious and labourious to follow, let alone to obey. It is therefore essential for believers to have the revelation of the ascended Christ who is the totality of God's heavenly economy.

The ascended Christ is now administering a monumental transitional epoch from the heavens and in man. A complete termination of the old with the germination of the new is a noticeable phenomenon recorded. The Apostles had to conceptualise and embrace this new reality but we see them struggling with old practises Acts 1:26. In the appointment of Matthias in replacement of Judas we see the Apostles casting traditional lots. Even in the present day Christianity a number of believers struggle with accepting this dispensational reality as they vacillate between the Old and New

Testament concepts. Hence contributing to a certain extent to the failure by a number of believers in appropriating their redemptive rights and privileges as articulated in the New Covenant.

The Pentecost

Acts 2:1, *"And when the day of Pentecost was fully come, they were all with one accord in one place".* The time had finally come as the Lord poured out His Holy Spirit on all the believers. It happened during the Feast of Weeks; which the Hebrews called **Pentecost** (Deuteronomy 16:10), fiftieth after the Passover on which the Lord was crucified (John 19:14). Pentecost was the fulfilment of the feast of weeks which was also called the feast of the Harvest (Exodus 23:16). The offering of a sheaf of the firstfruits was also a type of the resurrected Christ offered to God on the day of His resurrection (John 20:17) which was the day after the Sabbath (John 20:1) from that day to the day of Pentecost was exactly fifty days. What a fulfilment of prophecy? Jeremiah 1:12, *"....for I will hasten my word to perform it......"* The accuracy and precision in the fulfilment of prophecy is awesome.

The offering of Christ as the firstfruits in resurrection involves His secret ascension to the Father. When Mary wanted to touch Him, He said to her, *"Do not touch me, for I have not yet ascended to the Father ......"* John 20:17. This secret ascension was forty days prior to His public ascension in the sight of the disciples. He ascended to satisfy the Father.

As I have pointed out; the feast of Pentecost was the fulfilment of the feast of weeks which was also called the feast of Harvest. The feast of Harvest typifies the enjoyment of rich produce brought in by the resurrection of Christ. Not many Bible readers pay adequate attention to the harvest and that harvest typifies the enjoyment of all the riches of the resurrected Christ. The rich produce is actually the all-inclusive Spirit.

Do you know what exactly happened on the day of Pentecost? On this day there was an outpouring of the all-inclusive Spirit. The Spirit is the rich produce of the processed Triune God given to His chosen people as the blessing of the Gospel. Galatians 3:14, *"That the blessing of Abraham might come on the Gentiles through Jesus Christ; that we might receive the promise of the Spirit through faith".* This indicates that the unique blessing of the gospel is not the *"**eschatological heaven**"* but it is the enjoyment of the all-inclusive Spirit as the life giving Spirit (1 Corinthians 15:45). Dr. Poyer a renowned Researcher in Biblical Hermeneutics said, *"**Pentecost was the invasion of eternity into time.**"*

A Synopsis of the Impact of Pentecost

A) Dispensational Transfer

The completion of the dispensational transfer by Christ the Spirit is with immaculate precision. It brought to end the Old Testament religious practises and brought the new methodology of worship. Actually, I need to highlight that the book of Acts is very dispensational. The word "dispensational" is of course an adjective from the noun "dispensation". The reason the book of Acts is dispensational is that it describes a great transfer that was accomplished during a period of transition. This transfer from the Old Testament economy to the New Testament economy. I think it is important for me to explain the word economy to avoid interpretational confusion. Economy is an anglicised form of the Greek word *"Oikonomia"* which means dispensation. Hence dispensation and economy are synonyms, with dispensation the English equivalent of the Greek word *Oikonomia.* In the New Testament the *"Oikonomia"* denotes arrangement, government, management, administration and household. The word economy should therefore not pose any interpretational challenges as we proceed in the reading of this book in other chapters to follow.

In view of this dispensational transfer the old arrangement was altogether a matter of types, figures, shadows and prophecies which were not a reality. When the Triune God became a man in incarnation the transfer from shadow to reality began. The outpouring of the Holy Ghost was the "theological demarcation", though we see in the epistles time and time again the apostles themselves battling with a number of dispensational issues.

Through Pentecost – Christ breathed Himself to the entire humanity. Dr. Swiss says, *"Pentecost was a huge universal breath of Christ to humanity"*. *Eternal life became a reality.*

The formation of the new man – the corporate indwelling Christ, I Timothy 3:16, *"....God manifested in the flesh"*. The reality of the transfusion, infusion and transmission of God in man was and is being witnessed up to today. This is actually the validation and authentication of the doctrinal teaching on the "organic union", an interesting component of the new creation paradigm. Divinity infused or packaged in humanity as a result of the resurrection, ascension and descension of Christ the Spirit. Man in reality became the fleshy habitation of God as it was His eternal purpose from eternity past. From eternity past God planned and ordained the idea of dwelling in man. This we see portrayed choerographically in shadows, figures and types in the Old Testament e.g. the tabernacle of Moses. God through Christ the Spirit ceased to be an object of worship but became an intrinsically relational and subjective God. It is therefore important for the believers to be conscious of what they carry, this massive spiritual infrastructure called GOD in CHRIST the SPIRIT. This is awesome and it is a mystery, indeed, a great mystery according to scripture 1 Tim 3v16 In actuality, this is the fundamental basis for the doctrine on the *new creation ideology..* Our God is real and not a figment of imagination or fiction from social actors. He is life Deuteronomy 30 v20, 1 John 5 v11&12

Pentecost was in a way a replica of the phenomenon at Mount

Sinai when Moses was given the law by God. In this dispensation the new law was given by the ASCENDED Christ, as the Spirit. Chirst the Spirit became the indwelling reality. This was the reconfiguration, reconstitution and recalibration of man in relation to God's law. Jeremiah 31:33, *" But this shall be the covenant that I made with their fathers in the day that I took them by the hand to bring them out of the land of Egypt; which my covenant they brake, although I was an husband unto them, saith the LORD"*, Romans 8:2, *"For the law of the Spirit of life in Christ Jesus hath made me free from the law of sin and death"*. Now the law of the Spirit of life displaced the law of sin and death in the heart of a man. This brings transformation, sanctification and righteousness in the new man; the new creation. In actuality, this is the unveiled mystery and the sum total of redemption.

Pentecost brought in the universal accessibility of God by man through Christ. Romans 5:1-2, *"Therefore being justified by faith, we have peace with God through our Lord Jesus Christ. By whom also we have access by faith into this grace wherein we stand, and rejoice in hope of the glory of God"*. Dr. Mack Jones talks of ***"The mystery of Divine Ubiquity"***. The manifestation of God everywhere but more interestingly in man. The known communicable attributes of God, those qualities of His divine nature which although superlatively exemplified in Himself to a greater extent can be expressed in His people. Man became an expression through Christ the Spirit to His satisfaction. The moral qualities, which express God extensively and intensively such as holiness, goodness, wisdom, truth and love could manifest through man. This is an inward reality which should manifest outwardly as the fruit of righteousness in the reflection of Christ. 1 Peter 1:3, *"Blessed be the God and Father of our Lord Jesus Christ, which according to his abundant mercy hath begotten us again unto a lively hope by the resurrection of Jesus Christ from the dead"*.

B) Producing the Churches

Through the outpouring of the Holy Spirit, Christ gave birth to the formation of the church, the greatest mystery humanity had ever known. Practically, this was the universal enlargement and propagation of Christ. Propagation is a matter of production. To propagate is therefore to produce. The propagation of the resurrected Christ in His ascension produces the church. The churches are the produce of the resurrected and enlarged Christ in His ascension. The first mention of the word "Church" is in Acts 5:1. Thereafter the book of Acts speaks of the Church many times (8:1, 9:31, 11:22 and 26, 12:1, 13:1, 14:23, 15:3 and 20:17). In actuality, the Church produced by the resurrected Christ in His ascension is the Kingdom of God. On this let me hasten to say we should not listen to the teachings of some proponents of dispensationalism, who advocates that the Kingdom of God is no more. They claim it was suspended. This teaching is unscriptural and anti-Christ, should be discarded. These dispensationalist claim that the Kingdom of God will come after the Church age. In the book of Acts we see that the term Church and the Kingdom of God are interchangeably used depending on the context and application. In fact, the church is the Kingdom of God. With the book of Acts we have the Epistles which are essentially the continuation of the acts, of the Apostle for the edification of the saints so that the church may be fully built up as the Body of Christ. We are now the body of believers and the universal community of the saints in Christ.

C) Radicalisation of the Apostles

The Spirit at Pentecost resulted in the undeniable and irresistible "radicalisation" of the disciples as they carry the vision of preaching Christ and His kingdom. Acts 2:13, 22, 38, 41 says, *"....the same day three thousand were added unto them about three thousand soul".* One would not believe that this was the same fearful, and unstable

Peter preaching and declaring the Lordship of Jesus? They were spontaneously transformed from an apparently subdued entity to an aggressive, radical and spiritually militarised movement. They had received power for the demonstration of Christ. This is typically opposite of what happened at Mount Sinai. At Sinai about 3000 people died because of the law and at Pentecost 3000 people were given to the Spirit of life. This should be a reminder to believers that the law kills but the Spirit gives life. For this reason we realise in the Pauline writing the Apostle is radical and brutal when approaching matters concerning the Mosaic law.

Pentecost became a model of spirituality and the paragon of ethical integrity and fruitfulness. But the focus was not on the phenomenon but the man behind the phenomenon Christ Jesus the risen Messiah. All theological thoughts which followed started with the Spirit. Professor Akedi says, **"in light of Pentecost it is not far-fetched to call Christ Himself"**, **"the Pentecostal paradigm"**.

Dr. Honenberg said, **"Pentecost brought to rest all arguments and debates with regards to the integrity of Christ's historicity and Christology"**.

Dr. Marx Liberal says, **"Pentecost summarised Christology"**.

D) **The Perspectival Adjustment**

Pentecost brought in the "perspectival adjustment" with regards to the Kingdom message of Christ. The apostles would understand the message of Kingdom from eternal than earthly perspective, which was a complete shift from the previous dispensation.

Through Pentecost, the Apostle and even the church today witness the manifestation of the fulfilment of Jesus' prophecy, Mathew 16:18, *"....upon this rock I will build my church and the gates of hell shall not prevail against it.* This is the reality of the superimposition of Kingdoms and authority. The demonstration of the supremacy of Christ over the earthly kingdom. The shifting of kingdoms.

Pentecost was a localised phenomenon with far reaching universal impact, Christ the Spirit speaking to the entire universe. The universal verbalisation of God the Father through His Son.in resurrection.

This was a clear demonstration of the love of God in His pursuit to restore fallen humanity. Romans 5:5, *"And hope maketh not ashamed; because the love of God is shed abroad in our hearts by the Holy Ghost which is given unto us".*

The outpouring of the Holy Spirit was the outpouring of abundance of grace. The grace the apostle John in John 1:16, *"And of His fullness have all received grace for grace",* v 14*"......full of grace and truth".* Romans 5:17, *"For if by one man's offence death reigned by one; much more they which receive abundance of grace and of the gift of righteousness shall reign in life by one Jesus Christ".* Essentially Pentecost brought a new perspective in the definition and understanding of Grace. Grace is generally defined as unmerited favour though not inaccurate but superficial. Fundamentally, Grace is a person of Christ, the all-inclusive Spirit which has impacted and continue to impact generations positively. Christ is the embodiment of Grace. The mindset of the Apostles on grace changed drastically and radically. The message of grace became pivotal and stood as the pillar of truth in their preaching.

1 Timothy 3:15, *"....the pillar and ground of truth". .* **"Grace is not a dimensionless space or a theological ideology but a Person"** said Dr Matchtosh Bulls in one of his Theological Research papers.

E) **Hope Stimuli**

The Pentecostal experience was **"hope-inducing"**. Hope became a reality in the Person of Christ as they identified themselves with His Spirit in faith. Take note here the doctrine of identification. The principle of identification brings transformation hence the formation and the internalised imaging of Christ, who is express image of God. The Gospel became the message of hope not only to the Jews but the entire world. Despite political subjugation, persecution and harassment from the existing political establishment of the Roman Empire the apostles developed a sense of urgency and hope to preach Christ. In my view, the apostles emphasised Christianity as what I can call *"Eschatology in action"*. The soon coming Christ was in action demonstrating His power to humanity.

F) **Internalisation of Christ**

The Pentecost phenomenon resulted in the internalisation of Christ, the corporate and *"metabiological"* man. Christ became indwelling Spirit representing the God in the earth. The internalisation of Christ, the Spirit, essentially resulted in the *universal equalisation of man. We are equalised by the Spirit..* We now have the same image expressing the same God. No man is superior than the other in the Body of Christ. As recorded in Galatians 3: 28 '....*There is neither Jew nor Greek, there neither bond nor free there is neither male nor female; for ye are all one in Christ Jesus*'. We have the same Spirit in Christ. But, of course, the diversity of ministry gifts, offices and our God-given assignments should be respectably considered. At the same time it must be highlighted that our God has no respect of persons. (Acts 10:34)

G) **The Inspiration of the Scriptures**

The manifestation of the Spirit at Pentecost gave birth to New Testament scripture recordings and writings. Interesting to note is the distinction between God's **authorship and man's "penmanship"**, as in the mystery of incarnation. The mystery is that God spiritually connected Himself to humanity for the inspiration of Holy Scriptures. God made use of human channels, yet never surrendered His divine authorship or permitted the Book to become the word of man rather than His Word. God only used man for His inspirational purpose. II Timothy 3:16-17, *"All scripture is given* *by inspiration of God, and is profitable for doctrine, for reproof, for correction, for instruction in righteousness: That the man of God may be perfect, thoroughly furnished unto all good works"*. (2 Peter 1:21, 1 Thessalonians 2:13 and 1 Corinthians 14:37). The New Testament is made up of four main divisions in accordance with the masters' promise of a quadrilateral ministry of the Holy Spirit, which is evangelical, historical, polemical and prophetical. Here are terms of Jesus assurance, *"He shall testify of me"* (John 15:26, John 14:26, John 16:15). That is the revelation. It is the Spirit who illuminates the word. Dr. Khamer said; **"if we have lost the Spirit the authenticity and integrity of scripture becomes questionable"**. *"The letter killeth; but the Spirit giveth life"* 2 Corinthians 3:6.

Pre-Pentecost, it appears that the heavens were loaded with revelations and mysteries concerning God's eternal plan in Christ. The heavens were pregnant as the writer of the Ecclesiastes says on Chapter 11:3, *"if clouds be full of rain they empty themselves upon the earth…."* Pentecost triggered the heavens for God to pour out Himself on the earth for His full expression to His creation. Ecclesiastes 3:11, *"………… He has also set eternity in the heart of men……"* (NIV) Essentially, eternity had to burst for Christ to become an indwelling Spirit in man. Like Dr. Parker a renowned theologian said, *"….**God is a great believer in putting things down on a scroll or paper….**"* We have seen that while God is the Author of the Bible, He chose to collaborate in its production with some penmen. Emphasis must be on the fact that God reserves for Himself the prerogative of authorship. He does not violate or nullify the personalities of the **"secretaries of the Spirit"** that is the apostles.

Pentecost, was universally an impacting and cataclysmic phenomenon whose influence had far-reaching effects on generations to come. Isaiah 9:6, *"…..the government shall be upon his shoulder ….."* verse 7, *"of the increase of his government and peace, there shall be no end …."* By this ***splendiferous*** outpouring of the Holy Spirit we witness total restoration of dominion to man as we see the apostles exercising jurisdictional and governmental authority. Even the political establishments of the day were shaken. The divine influence of Christ globally spread unstoppably like veld fire until this generation. Kingdoms both in the natural and in the spirit realm were shaken to their foundation, until now the apostolic and prophetic aggression is on. Christ has to possess nations (Psalms 2:8). Christ be the Head of the regiment. (Ephesians 4:8, Acts 1:8, Isaiah 66:18 and Revelation11:15)

John the Baptist says in Luke 3:16, *"....He shall baptise you with the Holy Ghost and with fire"*. Acts 1:5, *"...but ye shall be baptised with the Holy Ghost not many days hence"* Acts 11:16, *"...but ye shall be baptised with the Holy Ghost"*. 1 Corinthians 12:*13 "For by one spirit are we all baptised into one body..."* The apostles were guided by the Holy Ghost. Actually, Pentecost paralysed Satan's insidious, nefarious and wicked machinery. The subtle and cheating Satan encountered a burning Christological reality. Satan himself is not omnipresent and his structures cannot cope universally with Christ as an indwelling Spirit in man. **Imagine 8 billon people carrying Christ the Spirit.** How can Satan win such a war? The reality is that he does not know on how to cope with this Great Army of Warriors in Christ who manifest themselves broadly across the globe. This is the splendour and awesomeness of the wisdom of God, *".....for had they known they would have not crucified the Lord of glory"*.

This revelation should give us courage to face any battle in this life knowing that in Him we are more than conquerors (Romans 8:37, II Corinthians 2:14). I believe in the "suddenlies of God" in Acts 2:2 was the biggest challenge the devil faced. He came face to face with his eternal destiny. He had to regroup his demonic troops for a new strategy. This "suddenly" is the manifestation of the Holy Ghost. Remember, as a believer there is a ***suddenly*** in every situation or challenge faced. The Lord in His Glory will appear suddenly to your deliverance. Through the ministration of the Holy Spirit Satan's evil machinations are set in disarray by the power of God. The Holy Ghost is the supreme strategist; the embodiment of the only wise God. Jude 25, *".....the only wise God our saviour ....."* Romans

16:27, *".....to God only wise be glory through Jesus Christ for ever"* 1 Timothy 1:17, *"Now unto the King eternal immortal, invisible, the only wise God, be honour and glory for ever and ever".* By the Spirit we witness the magnificent manifestations of the gifts of the Spirit. (1 Corinthians 12:1-10).

The outpouring of the Holy Ghost brought the ascended Christ on the earth as **"the gatherer of nations for God"** Christ the only one who rightfully qualifies for this designation. Isaiah 54:7, *"....with great mercies will I gather thee"* Matthew 12:30, *" gatherth not with me"* Mathew 23:37, *"O Jerusalem, Jerusalem, thou that killest the prophets, and stonest them which are sent unto thee, how often would I have gathered thy children together, even as a hen gathereth her chickens under her wings, and ye would not!".* Pentecost released Christ as the "universal cover" over God's people. Like the cloud that protected Israel in the wilderness. Our security and protection is in Him the resurrected, ascended and enthroned Christ who later descended as the Holy Ghost.

The Spirit of son-ship – one of the most outstanding significance of Pentecost is the ultimate manifestation.of Christ the Son of God to produce many sons for God on the earth for His expression as the Father of all. God from eternity past desired to have Himself expressed in a corporate way. He does not want simply an individual expression in the only begotten Son; but a body expression in many sons. John 1:18, *"No man hath seen God at any time; the only begotten Son, which is in the bosom of the Father, he hath declared him".* He declared, His intention was to make the only begotten Son the Firstborn among many brothers. Before resurrection of Christ; God had just one Son that is He had individual expression. But by resurrection which culminated into His ascension and descension; God now has a multitude of sons that is He has a corporate expression. ***The central function of the Holy Ghost is to produce sons, Son-ship is the ultimate.*** Romans 8:29, *".....you have received the spirit of adoption whereby we cry Abba Father". **"The supernatural outburst*** *of Pentecost precipitated a massive reproduction of the sons of God" Dr. Frasy Morrison.*

"Pentecost was the piercing of the womb of heavens to give birth to many sons of God" Dr. Stephens.

The release of the Spirit of Christ on the day of Pentecost brought in a new mindset among the followers of Christ particularly the Apostle. **"The unity paradigm"**. The Holy Ghost brought oneness among the saints. In typology, the Mosaic tabernacle is a picture of the genuine oneness for which the Lord Jesus prayed in John 17. The tabernacle was built with ***forty-eight boards*** that were overlaid with gold. These boards were held together by golden bars that ran through golden rings attached to the boards. In this way, the forty-eight boards became one. The wooden boards signifies humanity (the saints, the apostles) and the gold overlaying the boards signifies divinity. All the boards were overlaid with gold and connected by gold. This is genuine oneness. Romans 12:5, *"So we, being many, are one body in Christ, and every one member one of another".*

The Holy Ghost among believers is the unifying factor regardless of cultural, professional, social and political differences. The Holy Ghost immaculately embraces diversities in us but splendidly brings us to unity both for functionality and position in Christ. I am not writing as an advocate or proponent of ecumenicalism – the philosophy of the universal unity of the saints, but I am an aggressive proponent of unity in the faith of our Lord Jesus Christ. Ephesians 4:13, *"….the unity of the faith…."* I believe that believers might have methodological differences in articulating the message of Christ but the unity of the faith should remain a non-negotiable value. Psalms 133, *"Behold how good and pleasant it is for brothers to dwell together in unity…."* The Holy Spirit brings in believers the sense of unity, purpose and essentially a sense of belonging.

May GOD richly bless us and enjoy the privileges of the work of Christ.

Ten

The Gospel of God

Romans 1:1, *"Paul, a servant of Jesus Christ, called to be an apostle, separated unto the gospel of God"*.

Psalms 119:162, *"I rejoice at thy word, as one that findeth great spoil"*.

Over the years I have discovered that if there is something which is universally inevitable is change. Change can be positive or negative whichever way it still happens. Positive change in one's life is proportionate to knowledge one acquires. Knowledge makes the difference. In the academia there is a branch of philosophy referred to as phenomenology. This is a social science discipline which study and interpret phenomena (happenings). I actually enjoy, this academic discipline, However, over years of research and study I have discovered that none of the social scientists have managed to define change. In fact, they fail to understand that change or phenomena is directly linked to the Creator of the Universe. Everything in this world works according to His eternal purpose (Ephesians 1:11) Him who works out everything in accordance to the counsel of His will in conformity to His eternal purpose.

The bible, whose Authorship, GOD, has given it to us in its raw objective state. Therefore, His intention and objectivity has to be contextually investigated in order for us to establish our purpose in Him, Christ. Purpose in its essence is not only discovered but revealed.

1 Corinthians 2 v9-14"............*But God has revealed them*

unto us by the Spirit….." Glory is always in searching the unknown. Nearly every brand of religion is based on a book. Whether ancient or modern; mystical or historical ceremonial or ethical; it is almost certain to be founded on some allegedly sacred volume. That is supremely true of the Christian faith. It is, too based on a book the inspired theological document.

Matthew 13:52, *"Then said he unto them, Therefore every scribe which is instructed unto the kingdom of heaven is like unto a man that is an <u>householder</u>, which bringeth forth out of his treasure things new and old".* It has been always the desire of God from eternity past to talk to man in order to demystify His existence. And to do that we see in the Old Testament mostly He speaks in types which we call topology, numbers, numerology and parabolic language (parables). He could utter mysteries which would need the Spirit to interpret.

At the end of the chapter the Lord spoke an additional parable. Verse 52 after giving seven parables concerning the mysteries of the Kingdom, the Lord likened the instructed disciple or scribe to a ***householder*** who has treasure in a rich store; of things new and old, signifying not only new and old knowledge of the scriptures but also the new and old experiences of life in the Kingdom. This scribe mentioned here I believe was a scholar in the Old Testament who obviously knew the books of Moses and the prophets. Formerly, he was a scholar of the Old Testament dispensation but now he has been discipled into the Kingdom of the heavens. This means he has been discipled into this *new economy of God.* For this reason he likened him to a householder who bring forth out his treasure, things new and old. When the new are put together on the old we have precious and invaluable things. My deductive and exegetical analysis of this text is that the Lord here was possibly prophesying about the arrival of Apostle Paul well after His ascension. Apostle Paul could bring forth the old things and the new things from the vast resource base of his knowledge in Jewish religion, philosophy and law. We find out in the New Testament that Christ used him to bring out mysteries and consequently scribed two thirds of the New Testament which we now call the Pauline Epistles. He had rich in store and rich in treasure of knowledge. Out of his treasure; he could bring forth new and old doctrines, new and old experiences in an apostolic fashion which any other apostle could not. Apostle Peter, one of the nucleus of the original Jesus' Apostlic team commented years later in his epistles 2 Peter 3 v15 &16 that brother Paul"s writings are difficult to understand.

We now find out from the book of Romans Apostle Paul brings out an additional dimension in the revelation concerning Christ and His church. Most of us are accustomed to the four gospels, Matthew, Mark, Luke, and John, however, Apostle Paul brings in another perspective and dimension of the Gospel; *the Gospel of God.* Paul is adding by the Spirit of Christ another dimension to the gospel. *"Deep calleth unto deep...."* Psalms 42:7. This is the gospel which unveils the totality of new creation realities and that is the transmission or transfusion of divinity into humanity. The scriptural concept of the **organic union with Christ.** This unpacks the redemptive doctrines as ingeniously articulated in the New Testament. documentations.

When Jesus was on earth as the incarnate God, He would interact with man from outside man's environment but when He resurrected, ascended and descended as the Spirit, He is now inhabiting, indwelling, in man. *Fundamentally, man redemptively has become the habitat of God, the habitation of God and the vessel that contained God. This completely transformed the entire anthropological and sociological construct of Man. Athropologically man, a homosapien, that is emanating from human species became a homopneumaticus, implying, man is now interwovened with the Spirit. This theological concept undergirds the new creation paradigm.* This is, essentially, the Gospel of God, the reality of Christ as **the indwelling Spirit** as the embodiment of Grace. Apostle Paul is unveiling from the reservoir of his knowledge and treasure as Jesus prophetically spoke of in His parable in Matthew 13:52. This is the gospel in Romans, the gospel of God which focuses on Christ the indwelling Spirit, not the incarnate Christ, Christ in the flesh. This is the mystery of Godliness that God was made manifest in the flesh. This is the supremacy of His eternal wisdom which is far above principalities, powers and human rulers of this earth. This wisdom is far above any known epistemology, metaphysics or ontology. In Romans 8 we see that the Spirit of life which indwells is simply Christ Himself. Christ the ascended is in us as the governing Law of the Spirit of life. The Jesus in the four gospels was among the disciples but the Christ in Romans and the Epistles is within us. ***The Emmanuel, God with us is now the Emmanuel, God in us, the indwelling Spirit***. Resurrection, which ushered in Pentecost was instrumental in establishing this reality. As explained in the previous chapter Pentecost unbundled divine mysteries from eternity. This is something deep and more subjective than the incarnate Christ in the Gospels. *Hermeneutically, I don't think it would be an inaccurate biblical interpretation to assert that this fifth Gospel in the book of Romans is a crystallised and condensed choreograph of the mind of God on new creation, the new race, from eternity past now manifested in time.* The eternal purpose of God is systematically and doctrinally unpacked in this Gospel. A thorough study of this gospel gives us a further deeper insights in our understanding of the essence of the ***new creation paradigm***, which is a key focus of redemption. The understanding of our position in Christ is fundamentally underpinned on our understanding of this philosophy of new creationism. Now our Christ is higher more subjective and relational. We can relate with Him without any sophisticated spiritual protocol. He is the Spirit of life within us. He is such the subjective one. Though in John chapter 14 and 15 it is mentioned that Christ will abide in His believers but the pivotal aspect of the principle of the indwelling is fully expatiated in the Epistles particularly in Apostle Paul's writings.

Promised in the Scriptures

This Gospel was promised by God through the prophets in scriptures. Actually, this gospel was not accidental in its manifestation. The bible shows that this gospel was planned by God in eternity past. Before the foundation of the world God planned to have this gospel. So numerous times in the Holy Scriptures, from Genesis through to Malachi; God spoke through the prophets regarding this gospel. We see from the theology of the Mosaic tabernacle the vision and desire of God in His purpose to dwell in man. John 15:7, *"If ye abide in me, and my words abide in you, ye shall ask what ye will and it shall be done unto you."* Jesus in His teachings reiterated and expounded on this doctrine. **This gospel of God concerns in totality a Person, Christ and His capacity to inhabit man.** Of course, forgiveness, salvation etc are included in this gospel but they are not the central point. This gospel concern the indwelling Person of the Son of God, Jesus Christ our Lord. The wonderful person who has two natures – the divine nature and the human nature, divinity and humanity and He resides in a man, a corporal entity treasured by God. Paul mentions Christ's humanity and confirmed that He was born out of the seed of David according to the flesh (Romans 1:13). This is His human nature; His humanity.

Designated the Son of God out of Resurrection

Then Apostle Paul says He was, "designated the Son of God in power according to the Spirit of holiness out of resurrection of the dead" (Romans 1:4). This is clear reference to Christ's divinity. His humanity mentioned first and His divinity last. Paul mentions Christ's humanity first because he maintains the sequence of Christ's process. Firstly, Christ passed through the process of incarnation to become flesh. Then He passed through the process of death and resurrection. By means of the recorded steps of His processes He became the Son of God out of resurrection Christ has been processed into two steps – incarnation the second step death and resurrection. His first step brought Him to humanity. His second step brought man in divinity. This is a mystery displayed from ages past.Before incarnation Christ was already a Son of God (John 1:18). He was the Son of God before His incarnation and even Romans 8:3 says *"God sent His Son"*. Since Christ was already the Son of God before the incarnation; why did He need to be designated Son of God out of resurrection? Because by incarnation He had put on an element, the flesh, the human nature, that had nothing to do with divinity. By this resurrection Christ has sanctified and uplifted that part of His human nature; His humanity and He was designated out of this resurrection as the Son of God with human nature. So the bible says He was the begotten Son of God in His resurrection. He needed to be flesh to accomplish the work of redemption. **Redemption requires blood**. It is certain that divinity has no blood only humanity has blood and nevertheless redemption demanded blood. Hebrews 9:22, *"And almost all things are by the law purged with blood; and without shedding of blood is no remission of sin"*.

Essentially, the first step of His process was for redemption and the second step was for the impartation of life. Now we have the resurrected Christ within us as our life. The resurrected Christ as the Son of God is life to us. Whoever has the Son of God has life (1 John 5:12).

In Romans 8:2, we find the term "the Spirit of life". This is the indwelling Spirit. The indwelling Spirit is the Spirit of Christ and the Spirit of Christ is actually Christ Himself within us. Romans 8:9-10. This is, definitionally, the Gospel of God in its multi-grained dimensionality. This is the mystery of God hidden in Christ revealed in time from eternity. This is a mystery even to Satan and his demons cannot comprehend but to believers it is the revealed mystery. Christ, **through resurrection and Pentecost demystified God**. This is the most interesting truth revealed in this Gospel.

The Goal of the Gospel of God

This gospel is actually an exposition of the new creation, the corporate Christ, the last Adam. Through this Gospel the position of a believer is firmly anchored in Christ and the Word of God. The revelation of the finished work of Christ builds a strong foundation for our faith in God. This also facilitates our application of the Word into our journey into sonship in Christ.

With this understanding, inevitably a "perspectival adjustment" is realised in, the renewing of the mind, Romans 12:1-2, Jesus said in John 8:14, *"....for I know whence I came and wither I go ....." Our biblical psychology and philosophy changes as the revelation of our identity which defines our position in Christ increases. Position determines our inheritance and possesions.* This is treasure. This is the reason the devil would viciously want to fight the message of Grace. For Satan ignorance is his power base so he would strive to maintain it.

We see through this fifth Gospel Romans 1:3-4 gives us Jesus as the prototype. In Romans 8:29-30 we have many sons as the mass production. In this message we have talked about the prototype. With the prototype there is the Spirit of holiness, the flesh and the designation as the Son of God. Praise the Lord! We also have the Spirit of holiness within and the human flesh, so we are designated sons of God.

Son-ship; The Focus of the Gospel

The message on Son-ship is key and central to the revelation of Christ. We see the Apostle Paul talk about it over and over again in other epistles particularly Galatians 4 where he emphasises the need of a believer to be Spirit not Mosaic law conscious. Also to remember, is the fact that this gospel is powerful because the righteousness of God is revealed in it (Romans 1:17). According to John 3:16, salvation is out of God's love. According to Ephesians 2:8, salvation is by God's grace. But here in Romans, the epicentre of the Gospel of God, salvation does not only come out of the love of God or by the grace of God but salvation comes by the righteousness of God. This righteousness of God is revealed in the gospel out of faith and to faith, (Romans 1:17) meaning that as long as we have faith we have the righteousness of God, the righteousness of God comes out of our faith and to our faith.

We are established by this Gospel in righteousness. We are the righteousness of God in Christ. We are made the righteousness of God in Him, II Corinthians 5:21, *"For he hath made him to be sin for us, who knew no sin; that we might be made the righteousness of God in him."* It is important to note that righteousness and righteous living are different. Righteousness is given to us by God through Christ but righteous living come as a result of our walk with God in obedience to His word. Righteousness is supremely a unique subject on its own which is beyond the scope of the book.

Son-ship and the Church

In my article '**The Anatomy of the Church**' I endeavoured to give definitions of the church as articulated in the Bible. I considered it more appropriate in this book to include a portion explaining the interconnection between the church and son-ship in the Gospel of God.

What is the church? The church is a corporate composition of the brothers of the Firstborn Son of God. Assuming you remember the difference between the only begotten of Son of God and the First born Son of God. The only begotten Son of God had divinity without humanity. Although He had the divine nature, He did not have the human nature but the First born Son of God has both divine nature and human nature. The brothers who now constitute the church today are not the brothers of the only begotten but brothers of the First born son of God who came out of resurrection. Objectively and subjectively we are human and divine. The First born Son has humanity as well as divinity and all His brothers are the same as He is. We are a peculiar people. 1 Peter 2:9, *"But ye are a chosen generation, a royal priesthood, an holy nation, a peculiar people; that ye should shew forth the praises of him who hath called you out of darkness into his marvellous light".*

We were not a people but because of the grace of salvation through the redemptive processes in Christ we are now a people. 1 Peter 2:10, *"Which in time past were not a people of God...."* Now do you realise whose son you are? You are God's son. God is our divine Father and we are all His divine sons because we all have been born of His divine life with His divine nature. We are the many sons of the Father and many brothers of the Firstborn Son of the Father. In actuality, the church is supremely both human and divine living organism. This is the nature of the church a composition of the many sons of God. To put it correctly the church is not a cathedral, chapel or physical sanctuary or a physical infrastructure but a gathering of the called ones. It the "ekklesia" a community of believers in Christ. The church of Jesus Christ is the **"Divine Masterpiece"** Dr. Rosey Thomas.

We do not have much space to write in detail all the definitions of the church but the following scriptures are relevant to add knowledge on the subject;

Mathew 16:18, Acts 2:44 and 47, Acts 4:32, Acts 15:14, 1Corinthians 16:19, 1Corinthians 12:28, Ephesians 1:22-23, Ephesians 3:10 and 21, Ephesians 4:11-12, Colossians 1:18, Hebrews 12:22-23 and Rev21:2

Eleven

The Gospel of the Glory of God

Isaiah 51:16, *"**And I have put my words in thy mouth**, and I have covered thee in the shadow of mine hand, that **I may plant the heavens,** and lay the foundations of the earth, and say unto Zion, Thou art my people."*

Rev 1:12-16, *"And I turned to see the voice that spoke with me. And being turned, I saw seven golden candlesticks; **And in the midst of the seven candlesticks one like unto the Son of man**, clothed with a garment down to the foot, and girt about the paps with a golden girdle. His head and his hairs were white like wool, as white as snow; and his eyes were as a flame of fire; And his feet like unto fine brass, as if they burned in a furnace; and his voice as the sound of many waters. And he had in his right hand seven stars: and out of his mouth went a sharp two edged sword: and his countenance was as the sun shineth in his strength."*

In the previous chapters we talked about the four Gospels, the Gospel of God and now we discussing the The Glory of the Gospel. All these distinctions of the Gospel are important because they give us a variety of perspectives on how God the Father expects us to function in the Church and this earth. . .

The subject of the finished work of Christ has to be emphasised over and over again because of its pivotal nature to our understanding of entire Christology which has to shape our theology of this true God. Now that we understand that He has resurrected, ascended and descended as Christ the Spirit we should be conscious of the operations of the Holy Spirit as He reveals the mystery of the Father and His kingdom? As a result of the outpouring of the Holy Ghost at Pentecost, the eternal Christ has **"Tabernacled"** among us and in us as the Word and the Spirit. I believe we are the generation to witness the fulfilment of the feast of tabernacles as we await for the final and total fulfilment of the endtime prophecies. The full manifestation of the millennium kingdom. Therefore, as believers we do not need to wait to enjoy the fruits of the finished work of Christ in by and by in the distance eternal future. In our journey to understand Christ through His holy scriptures we have noticed that His immanency through Pentecost has overshadowed His transcendence. As stated previously that, the main aspects of redemption that is incarnation, crucifixion, resurrection, ascension and Pentecost inevitably amplified His immanency and accessibilty, Emmanuel, the God with us, is now the God in us, He is objectively on the throne in the heavens, and also subjectively indwelling by the Spirit in the hearts of man. I am always impressed by the poetic writing of the Prophet Isaiah chapter 51:16. The inference in the scripture is that God has put His word on the lips of His servant to proclaim and as they proclaim they *"plant the heavens"* in the earth, which is in reality the manifestations of His kingdom. ***The ethereality of God becomes a reality on the earth and the operation of the Holy Ghost, the Spirit of Christ is more pronounced.*** The expectation of God is that.heaven should be a reality on the earth. The truth is that Man should not yearn for heaven instead should enjoy heaven on the earth. This is, essentially, His eternal purpose from the beginning in eternity past. This then should potentially discount the **heaven theology**, which is so popular particularly among the evangelicals. **In my own analysis it is actually low mindedness and parochial to have a goal of going to heaven. Christ who is above the heavens should be our individual or corporate vision.**

In Rev 1:12-16, we see the ascended one on the centre of the throne of God and the universe. We see Christ on His administration of the universe administrating God's eternal purpose among the churches as He exercises His priestly care for churches. Christ is revealed as the Son of man (*corporeality*) clothed in the robe of His High Priest. Professor J. Lason in his theological article on, ***Eternity Demystified,*** said," ***Christ's corporeality demystifies his ethereality as His universal accessibility became an experiential reality.***"

In Rev 1:16, we see Christ described, *"…..and out of his mouth went a sharp twoedged sword….."* This is His word which he uses to administer the purpose of God on the throne. It is vitally important for us to note that God moves in the universe by speaking His Word Heb 1:3, *"….upholding all things by the word of his power ……."* His Word with its supernaturality has the power to maintain the existing universal order Dr John Motton said ",………**The universe and creation as a whole will cataclysmically collapse without His Word. This is an inconceiveable reality and it is beyond human comprehension.** Geo-scientists and Creationists may have their theoretical opinions on this subject but the truth about our Sovereign God is not subject to debate but stands un altered. Like in the ancient days the decree or signature of a King could not be changed. **There is power in His Word**. This is the reason why Apostle John in Rev 19:10 describes Jesus Christ on the throne as, *"Spirit of prophecy"*. But, of course, as I have highlighted in the previous chapters, that the word of God should be the benchmark in testing all spirits to safeguard ourselves against the spirit of anti-Christ which is in operation in the world.

Over a couple of years a huge industry has sprung up around prophecy, As a result of biblical illiteracy, poverty, spiritual gullibility and immaturity the gift of prophecy has been horrendously abused in the Church fraternity. Therefore, the Word should help us in maintaining the much needed spiritual order and balance in the church.

"The unfolding of thy word gives light" says the Psalmist (Psalms 119:130). There is unfathomable depth of revelation we have not yet realised in God's word, even concerning the most fundamental doctrines. It is a terrible mistake to become satisfied with our present

knowledge and understanding. We are seeing through a glass darkly. We cannot know anything fully until we know Him fully. Proverbs 4:18, *"But the path of the just is as the shining light, that shineth more and more unto the perfect day."*

Therefore, the importance of prophecy cannot be underestimated. Prophecy leads to the revelation and manifestation of Christ. In the book of Ezra 6 v14 we read that as the Jews elders were rebuilding the Temple, they were empowered, inspired and encouraged by the prophesying of Haggai and Zechariah the leading prophets of the time. Essentially, as believers our destiny and our spiritual journey is undergirded by the prophetic. The Old Testament prophets saw into the future and spoke primarily about the coming of the Messiah and His kingdom. This is powerfully illustrated in the story of the two men on their way to Emmaus. While these two were on their way home, they were in deep discussion about the just past crucifixion, apparently perplexed, dejected, and vividly demoralised. At that point Jesus joined them on the road and surprised them by asking questions about their discussion as if he did not know what they were talking about. Of course, their eyes were prevented from recognising Him. After listening to their version and explanation of the events that had taken place, Jesus finally opened their eyes through reading to them the Word. Beginning with Moses and with all the prophets he explained to them the things concerning Himself in all the scriptures. The lesson here is that when ministering the Word we should focus on those aspects of the Bible which brings out the expression *"**concerning Himself**"*. Which is also highlighted by God in Exodus 19 v4" *.........and brought you to myself"*. We see here an insight into His eternal purpose. To bring back Man to **HIMSELF**. If it is prophecy, the motivation must be to lift Jesus not man. The epicentre should be Christ and His Word not man. Ministers of the word should not attract people to themselves but to Christ. Mature sons of God need a balanced approach towards the Word. Ministers of the Word should not behave like celebrities in seeking for fame and recognition by drawing attention of people to themselves. This is deception which should not be part of the body of Christ. It is the **spirit of Diotrephes**, which seeks for pre-eminence at the expense of Christ. 3 John v9. Such, has no respect from scriptures and should therefore be vehemently condemned.

The Scene in Heaven after Christ's Ascension

Most Christians know that Christ has ascended into heaven and that he is in heaven and in us today. However, not many are familiar with the scene in heaven after Christ's ascension. This scene is quite particular, and we need to see it very clearly.

Rev 4:1, *"After this I looked, and, behold, **a door was opened in heaven**: and the first voice which I heard was as it were of a trumpet talking with me; which said, Come up hither, and I will shew thee things which must be hereafter".*

God's plan is hidden in Christ in the heavens. When God finds a man after His own heart on the earth the heaven is opened to him. It was opened to Jacob (Genesis 28:12-17) to Ezekiel (Ezekiel 1:1) to Jesus (Mathew 3:16) to Stephen (Acts 7:56) and to Peter (Acts 10:11). Here and Rev 19:11, heaven is opened to John, the writer of the book of Revelation and heaven has to be opened to all believers in the Lord in eternity now and fully in the future (John 1:51) as we engage the Spirit of Christ. It must be noted with interest that God is so obsessed with revealing Himself to whosoever makes a deliberate and intentional decision to seek His face, because He is not far away from His people because of the reality of His immanency. A culture of prayer has to be emphasised time and time again.

The horns of the altars should not be cut off like prophet Amos said in Amos 3 v14 The cutting of the horns of the altar is essentially a metarphoric expression of prayerlessness.

The book of Revelation gives us a distinct and panoramic view of the scenes in the heavens after Christ's ascension than any of the books in the Bible. This book is not a book of eccentric symbols, images, frogs, animals, serpents and scorpions etc. But it is the full revelation of Christ and the church. Here Christ is the witness (Revelation 1:5), the testimony is the expression of God, and the church is the testimony; the expression of Christ. As such the church is the reproduction of the testimony, the expression of God in Christ. Space-wise His administration is universal and time-wise it is eternal.

Now the Son is on the throne as King of kings and the Lord of lords (Revelation 19:16). The King of kings refers to authority and the Lord of Lords refers to His headship. It is important to note that this description we find here is essentially our position in Christ and we should exercise authority from this position as the sons of God. He is the authority and the Head of the universe. He is the Lion of the tribe of Judah (Revelation 5:5) and the Lamb (Revelation 5:6, 21:23 and 22:1).

The Opening of the Secrecy of God's Administration by the Lamb

Revelation 5:1, *"And I saw in the right hand of him that sat on the throne a book written within and on the backside, sealed with seven seals."*

God's administration is a secret and a mystery. Christ is the one sitting on the throne has a scroll in His hand sealed with seven seals. The seals are actually the contents of the scroll and contents of the book of Revelation, for this book is the opening of the unveiling of the seven seals. ***The scroll itself must be the new covenant; the grand title deed enacted with the blood of the Lamb.*** The new covenant is a scroll covering the redemption of church; Israel, the world and the universe. When Christ died on the cross, He tested death not only for man; but for everything (Hebrews 2:9).

Now, after Christ's ascension, there should no longer be a secret, for it has been unsealed by Christ death, resurrection and ascension. He has fulfilled God's requirements. Christ is worthy to open the seals, the mysteries of God. No one was worthy before the cross but now Christ is qualified to open the seals and the scrolls. Rev 5:2-4, *"And I saw a strong angel proclaiming with a loud voice₁ **Who is worthy to open the book**, and to loose the seals thereof? And no man in heaven, nor in earth, neither under the earth, was able to open the book, neither to look thereon. And I wept much, because no man was found worthy to open and to read the book, neither to look thereon"*, Revelation 6:1, *"And I saw when the Lamb opened one of the seals, and I heard, as it were the noise of thunder, one of the four beasts saying, Come and see."*

The opening of the seals by the Lamb transpired immediately after Christ's ascension to the heavens. Through His incarnation, crucifixion and resurrection; Christ is fully qualified in His ascension to open the mystery of God's economy which is contained in the seven seals.

A Four-Horse Race

The first four seals comprise four horses with their riders in a four horse race. All four riders are not real persons but personified things. It is evident that the rider of the second horse; the red horse, is war (verse 4) and the rider of the third horse, the black horse is famine (verse 5) and the rider of the fourth horse the pale horse is death (verse 8). I believe according to historical facts the rider of the first horse the white horse; must be **the Gospel of Glory** not as some theologians interpret as Christ or the anti-Christ. Interesting to note immediately after Christ's ascension, these four things – the gospel, war, famine and death began to run like riders on four horses and will continue, I believe until Christ comes back. Beginning with the first century the gospel has been spreading throughout all these twenty centuries. War has been also proceeding simultaneously. War always causes famine and famine death. All these will continue until the end of the age.

Interpretation: Rider of the White Horse

The rider of the white horse is *the preaching of the gospel.* White obviously signifies purity, cleanness and approvability. Rev 6:2, *"And I saw, and behold **a white horse:** and he that sat on him had **a bow; and a crown** was given unto him: and he went forth conquering and to conquer".* A bow is for fighting with an arrow. But here there is a bow without an arrow. This indicates that the arrow has already been shot to destroy the enemy and victory has been won for the constitution of the gospel of peace. Now the fighting is over and the gospel of peace is proclaimed. On the cross, the arrow was shot into the heart of the enemy. The battle was fought and victory has been won. II Corinthians 2:14, *"Now thanks be unto God, which always causeth us to triumph in Christ, ...".* Verse 2, *".......a crown was given to him".* A crown is a sign of glory. *The Gospel has been crowned with the glory of Christ.* II Corinthians 4:4 speaks of the *"glorious gospel or the gospel of the glory Christ".* The gospel we preach is the gospel crowned with glory of Christ. Therefore, in inference, the gospel we preach is the gospel of glory not only the gospel of grace or the gospel of God. It is a conquering gospel in dealing with all opposition forces.

We Access the Open Heaven with this Gospel

This gospel of the glory of Christ has in it elements of self-revelation, self-validation and self-qualifying. It does not need man to improvise power for it. It is the power of God and the manifestation of the Spirit of Christ. If this gospel is incarnated in the spirit man it becomes experiential and has the capacity to open the heavens for the saints. The incarnation of this gospel in man brings deliverance and anointing. Anointing, refers to the empowerment with multiple capacities given to man for a varied functionalities. It is more than just the smearing with oil on the forehead of the believer but it is an inward dynamo-like drive in the spirit a of man. The closer you are to this gospel the faster the heavens open for the manifestation of His Glory, for He is the God of glory. Like an automated door, it only open when you step closer to it. This is the gospel of peace which the world cannot give.

The Gospel of the glory of Christ is the gospel which brings the manifestation of the sons of God. Romans 8:19. The sons of God have to be revealed for this is the eternal purpose of God. The preaching of this gospel will precipitate His coming back for the second time. The ground work for His coming back is being prepared by the preaching of this gospel. I believe this is the gospel the Lord Himself spoke of in the book of Mathew 24:14, *"And **this gospel of the kingdom** shall be preached in all the world for a witness unto all nations; and then shall the end come"*. This gospel shall be preached in the whole inhabited earth for a testimony to all nations and the end shall come. This is the main reason there is an accelerated pace now in the preaching of the gospel of the kingdom world over, because the world is rapidly unfolding the coming to an end of this age. But before the consummation of the age Christ *"the desire of all nations shall be manifested"* Haggai 2:7 has to be preached in the whole world.

As we see the historical narrative of Joseph's life as he related to his brothers in Genesis 45:1, *".......Joseph made himself known unto his brethren"*. This is the eternal desire of God for Christ to be known to the Church and the entire creation. The redemption narrative cannot be a complete historical document without the revelation of Christ to His brothers, the redeemed community. This is the mystery of the eternal plan of God. As pointed out in the previous chapters, Christ is transcendental and yet immanent. He is outside the cosmic and yet accessible and close to His creation. This is the glory of Christ's gospel. **The glory of God is in the unknown.** The hidden has to be revealed that is glory. Proverbs 25:2, *"It is the glory of God to conceal a thing: but the honour of kings is to search out a matter"*. As believers we need to be diligent in searching the revelation of Christ in His word for His glory to be manifested. We are as a Church expected to be the embodiment of His glory.

Manifestation of His Glory

Briefly, before concluding this chapter I feel it is imperative to touch on the subject of glory. **What is glory?** In theology, the term Glory is referred to ***doxa, from doxologia in Greek*** the weight of a substance. Without being too technical and theologically intricate, a simple definition of glory is that it is the manifestation of the character and nature of a thing. Glory is intrinsic but with extrinsic value. We need to have a new mindset on the way we appreciate glory. We need to do away with the traditional concepts which define glory as some form of radiant, emission, or lighting, though occasionally God might desire to show up in this manner. But more precisely, glory is an accurate and correct representation of a thing. **In the case of the redeemed we have glory intrinsically inherent in us because of the Holy Spirit.** It is in seed form and to be manifested in its true nature sometimes with the process of time or the fullness of time to its maturity. Just as the Lord says, you are the light of the world. He speaks in ***an anthropomorphic language but simple. Anthropomorphism i***s using natural images to describe divine things of God e.g. the hand of the Lord, the lips, the eyes and the finger etc. All these are anthropomorphic expressions, it does not imply that God has lips, hands and so on because God, in essence is Spirit (John 4 v24). Therefore, we cannot understand Him from a physical perspective.

The Lord is not saying we are the light, so we should be like small bulbs shining like fire in the dark. He is basically talking of our accurate representative position. If believers correctly represent God on the earth, this is glory, the expression of Himself in His creation. This is the reason Christ in some portions of scriptures He is called, *"......the Lord of glory"* I Corinthians 2:8. The gospel of the glory

Christ has in it the capacity to transform a man and reposition him to accurately represent God – **this is the essence of His Glory *and fundamental to His Eternal Purpose.***

The New Testament tells us that we have been called into glory and that this glory was designed according to God's wisdom in eternity past. I Corinthians 2:7, *"But we speak the wisdom of God in a mystery, even the hidden wisdom, which God ordained before the world unto our glory".* Both I Thessalonians 2:12 and 1 Peter 5:10 tell us that we have been called into this glory. And according to Colossians 3:4 when Christ appears we shall appear with Him in glory.

Actually, we may illustrate this matter of glory by the example of a sunflower. The seed of the sunflower is very small. If you sow the seed on earth, it will grow until it eventually reaches the blossom stage. When this sunflower blossoms that is the glorification. A long process must transpire from the seed stage to the blossoming stage. As the sunflower passes through this process it must fight in many ways to survive. Just like your life as a believer, you fight difficult circumstances until you conquer and come to blossoming stage. Its blossoming is its glory. Every one of us without exception is like a sunflower seed. Through regeneration, the life of glory has come in to us. We now have a seed of glory within us. This life that we have within us as a seed is the life of glory. This is Christ in us the hope of glory. (Colossians 1:27)

Therefore, glory as I said; is not merely a small radiant shining in the air. That is too objective. If glory were merely an outwards shining, it would simply be another vanity. But that is not the glory that the bible reveals or talks about. The glory revealed in the Bible is the very blossoming of God's divine element in us which essentially gives us the ability to perfectly represent God in the earth. The principle of perfect representation must be appreciated.

Consider the transfiguration of the Lord Jesus at the mountain top (Mathew 17:1-2) when the Lord ascended to the top of that mountain and was transfigured. Did the Shekinah glory suddenly come upon Him from outside from the third heavens? Did He enter into an outward shining or brightness? No the glory shone from within Him. That is why it is called transfiguration. Likewise the glory into us shall be brought out is the very glory that is within right now. It is not merely objective but subjective.

In regeneration, a life element comes into our being. This life element is not small thing. It is God's divine element. All that God is, is the substance; this is life element that has come to our being. We all must realise what happened when we were regenerated. God's divine element came in to us.

When the children of Israel entered Canaan they began to blossom. That was their glory. That blossoming stage was also a fight stage, for they began to fight almost immediately after entering the land of Canaan. Their first battle they fought was at Jericho. After Jericho, they fought continually until David defeated all the enemies and the temple was built. Then the glory of God filled the temple (1 Kings 8:10) apparently the glory that filled the temple came down from above, actually the glory was with the children of Israel. Since the day they crossed the Red Sea the glory was with them. The glory was in the pillar of cloud and pillar of fire. (Exodus 14:19-20). When they built the temple, the temple was filled with glory. Again, the glory did not come from above. It was present already, waiting for the people's growth and development in maturity. When the children of Israel were fully grown the glory filled the temple. In actuality, maturity is the gateway to heirship. **Maturity, from various researches carried out is the major ingredient lacking in the operational systems of the present day church.**

Likewise, we all had a beginning at the time of our regeneration. It was our Passover (the cross), since that time when the seed of glory was sown into us; that seed has been growing. We entered His glory on the day of resurrection. Luke 24:26 indicates that Christ entered into glory not by ascending but by resurrection. His resurrection was His entry into glory and He led many sons to His glory. And on the day of Pentecost He fully manifested His glory by the outpouring of the Holy Ghost. Essentially, we live in glory and the joy of the Lord is to see to it that we manifest this glory for His satisfaction.

It is important to note that this glory has been in Christ before the foundation of the world John 17:5, *"And now, O Father, glorify thou me with thine own self with the glory which I had with thee before the world was"*. And as we were in Christ also before the foundation of the world we also had this glory from eternity past. Our understanding of this revelation of the glory of Christ should enhance our appreciation of the finished work of Christ. Actually, the reality is that this glory is the finished work of Christ. We need to live in this reality. This is the main reason that the Christian faith is higher in its standard than other faith in the world.

II Corinthians 3:18, *"But we all, with open face beholding as in a glass the glory of the Lord, are changed into the same image from glory to glory, even as by the Spirit of the Lord"*.

This glory mentioned here by the apostle is not a dimensionality in impression but the realisation of the revelation of the New Testament glory in Christ. The totality, centrality and unveiling of Christ's redemptive accomplishments. It is the glory in Christ; our inheritance. All the ceremonies, festivals, ritualistic sacrifice collapsed in Christ. Christ is the centre and focus of the eternal purpose of God. The reality of this revelation is liberating and inspiring and it has to be embraced by every believer worthy His calling. This glory makes us higher in value than angles and the devil knows this and envies. We are the mystery revealed and our destiny as the community of believers is New Jerusalem the city of God. **This is the consummation of all His Glory, His Glory, Glory to God.**

It is advantageous for a believer to be always connected to the leading of the Holy Spirit for the glory to be manifested. The Holy Spirit is the embodiment of Christ's glory in the heavens and in us. We are the carriers of this seed of glory. Isaiah 53:10, *".......he shall see his seed, he shall prolong his days, and the pleasure of the Lord shall prosper in his hand"*

On the throne Christ is watching over his seed to prosper in manifesting the glory of the Father in heaven and in us. He is administering the word of the Father for its fulfilment. The fulfilment of the word, the prophetic word, is the manifestation of His glory. All what was written and what is being spoken as the present truth concerning Christ has to be fulfilled. This is His glory. The reason God watches over His word to perform is that He wants His glory to become a reality to His creation." **2 Thessalonians1:10............................to be glorified in the saints.............."**

Interesting to note is that all the challenges, the trials and temptations we sometimes go through are for His glory to be manifested. You are called to fellowship with Him and be a splendid display of His glory. I am impressed by the raising of Lazarus by Jesus in John 11. He says to Martha in verse 40, *".....if thou wouldest believe, thou shouldest see the glory of God".* Take note of the expression, the *"glory of God".*

The bible says in James 1:2, *"....count it all joy when ye fall into diver temptations".* Why should you celebrate when you are going through pain? It is for the manifestation of His glory. Why was Joseph thrown into the pit and eventually sold to slave handlers who took him to Egypt? It was for the glory of God to be manifested. Genesis 45:13 Joseph said *"and ye shall tell my father of all my glory in Egypt".* Take note of the expression again *"...glory".* I believe sometimes certain situations are allowed by God in our lives for His glory to be manifested. But all these things we triumph in Christ (II Corinthians 2:14). Many examples I can illustrate on this subject of glory in us but what is more important and pivotal is to know that we are the epitome of the manifestation of His glory on the earth. II Corinthians 4:17, *"For our light affliction, which is but for a moment, worketh for us a far more exceeding and eternal weight of glory",* again take note of the expression *"....***eternal weight of glory***".* We are redeemed for His glory so we need to be conscious of this glory in us. The bible says, *"**out of his belly shall flow rivers of living water**"*

John 7:38. Intentionally, therefore, allow the flow of His glory from within you to flow out, that is to be manifested. In the book of Exodus 33 v18 we hear the prayer of Moses to God. *"Lord show me your glory." The quest for glory should be a daily request to God*

Dr S.V. Simmons, said ",...The outburst of eternity into time on the day of Pentecost was essentially a manifestation of His Glory. Experientially, Pentecost must be a daily phenomenon in the life of a believer."

Ezekiel 47: 1 *"....waters issued from under the threshold of the house eastwards ...."* Note here in this verse, the waters came out of the temple. The Spirit of God has a mandate to manifest the glory of the Father. We are the temple of God. 2 Corinthians 6:19, *".... your body is the temple of the Holy Ghost..."* In Ezekiel 47:18, the water goes down into a desert. The dying world needs healing through the Gospel of Glory. The Spirit of God which is resident in us needs to come out from within us, the temple, which we are, the strength, the rule-ship and the influence of Christ on earth. This is His Glory. The Glory of God brings life to the dead and the virtually dead situation. The eccelesiological and missiological mindset of Christ has to be the central message on our pulpits for His Glory to be revealed. In the earth, Christ has to be exalted on earth through the preaching of this glorious gospel which is unparalleled. Lives have to be restored, sinners have to be saved. Precisely and essentially, this gospel of the glory of Christ should be the solution to this disillusioned, frustrated, dying and rejected world. The Spirit of Christ which is the Spirit of the word should not only be prominent in the temple, but must have influence and resonance outside the temple. The world is in a desperate state and we as a church need to adopt desperate measures to carry the mandate of the gospel. We are His instrument for change.

Isaiah 51:20. *"Thy sons have fainted, they lie at the head of all the streets, as a wild bull in a net: they are full of the fury of the Lord, the rebuke of thy God."*

Dr. Lawson said, **"God is hamstrung if man does not move,**

the cooperation of man with God brings the desperately needed change in the world."

Can you be the colt or "donkey" that Christ can use for His purpose? Christ is looking for a vessel to use for the world to shout *"Hosanna; blessed is that which cometh in the name of the Lord"*. Mark 11:10, *"....Hosanna in the Highest."* The world in its hopeless state desperately needs the message of hope. *You are His battle axe and weapon of war."* This is the essence of the gospel of glory of the God. The focus of this gospel is building and giving life, not theatrical drama and performances common among the saints today. The glorious Christ must take centre-stage.

As we search through scriptures, it is also interesting to note that wealth and riches are also equated to glory. This is not in the scope of the book but to be discussed in other editions to come.

Twelve

God's Eternal Purpose – the Expression of Christ

Over the years, we have learnt to experience the transforming and building life of Christ is not an overnight phenomenon (event) but a process which is sometimes cumbersome and uncomfortable to the carnal mind. In the seven epistles to the churches in the book of revelation there are many difficult verses e.g. Rev 3:12 where the Lord said, *"He who overcomes, I will make him a pillar in the temple of my God and the name of the city of my God, the New Jerusalem which descends out of heaven from my God and my new name".* When I read this statement of verses, a couple of years ago I could not understand its implications. It came to the realisation that our faith journey is a journey into the fulfilment of His promises. The bible as our manual for life is replete of promises connected to **The *Promise***, Christ. In Revelation two and three there is the promise of the Lord to the overcomer in the Church of Philadelphia one of the seven Churches discussed in the book of Revelation. Essentially, studying this book should definitely help us to discover our eternal purpose in God through Christ.

The Lord's promise here is not so to give us something but to make us into something. According to our concept, *a promise is related to a blessing in most cases something physical in nature.* To us, without a blessing, there can be no promise. But Rev 3:12 the Lord did not say, *"I will give him",* He said, *"I will make him".* In this verse the Lord did not promise to give us holiness as a heavenly blessings, material blessing, cars, mansions etc no here He promises to make us become something – **a pillar in the temple of God.** Becoming a pillar in the temple of God involves two things, transformation and building. After new birth follows transformation to confirm to the image of Christ for the main purpose that is to express God on earth Fundamentally, identification effect transformation. Romans 8:29, *"For whom he did foreknow, he also did predestinate to be conformed to the image of his Son, that he might be the firstborn among many brethren",*

II Corinthians 3:18, *"But we all, with open face beholding as in a glass the glory of the Lord, are changed into the same image from glory to glory, even as by the Spirit of the Lord".*

We have to be ready for the Lord to transform us to become a pillar. This is truly the greatest blessing which we believe is connected to the blessing of Abraham in Galatians 3:14, *"That the blessing of Abraham might come of the Gentiles through Jesus Christ; that we might receive the promise of the Spirit through faith".* We believe the blessing of Abraham has been misrepresented in church to mean largely material things. Material things, of course, cannot be dismissed but are not fundamentally the basis of this blessing. The blessing of Abraham is the forgiveness of sin in redemption of mankind and the ultimate making of Abraham the full expression of God on the earth which has been degraded into idol worship occultism, spiritism and other forms of mythology. We see that the greatest blessing is for the Lord to make us like God, to make us an expression of Christ. Perfect representation is what God is looking for in man. Creation needs to know who is this intriguing figure called God. Man is the corporeal entity to reflect who God is on the earth. God desires to see Himself in Man. The Church must therefore see the Lord's greatest blessing which is to make us become something. The way in which He accomplishes this is to work Himself into us. The writing of the name of God, the name of the New Jerusalem and the new name of the Lord upon us actually refers to the working of God in us and to the working of the attributes of Christ into us as His new creation. Therefore, the greatest blessing in the Church life is not that the Lord will give us something but that He is now working Himself into us to make us a part of the New Jerusalem. In eternity future, we even now enjoy the benefits of the eternity present. All this is a function of the Spirit. Through this working, we may have something of God as well as some experience of the all-inclusive Christ. Obviously, we know that material blessings are a by-product of the centric blessing, Christ the Spirit. Although the Lord promises to take care of us, we do not consider the outward care to be much of the real blessing. The true blessing is that He is making us a pillar in the temple of God for perfect representation. It has been the desire of God in His eternal purpose to make us His habitation. From this perspective we see that our **"blessing theology"** has to be redefined or upgraded to become more Christ-like. Ephesians 2:21-22, *"In whom all the building fitly framed together growth unto a holy temple in the Lord: In whom ye also are builded together for an habitation of God through the Spirit"*.

The essence, the substantial element of the habitation, the house of God is not divinity but humanity. Divinity is the dweller and humanity is the dwelling. Since the house is the building place and not the dweller, the dwelling is humanity and the dweller is divinity. Thus humanity, however is not a natural or a created humanity, it is a regenerated, transformed and uplifted humanity, a humanity that has been processed through the, incarnation, crucifixion, resurrection and ascension of Christ. A humanity which has passed through such processes becomes the very substance of God's building. Such a humanity is God's dwelling place. Actually, this is the sum total of redemption, God, divinity packaged in humanity to express His love. In eternity past Christ had only divinity but in eternity future Christ will have both divinity and humanity forever. The children of God are the expansion and enlargement of God for His corporate expression. The only begotten Son of God is God's declaration, making Him to all the people who enjoy God"s fullness as grace and reality. The children of God are many and are the expression of God. We are the children of God, born of the Spirit to express God on earth.

For years, even today in Christianity you can hardly hear a word about God"s building. Many understand the word building; taking it to mean the same as edification. For many, to build up is simply to edify. Although, many stress edification, not much is talked about on practical building of the Church of God. Nevertheless, what is the ultimate consummation of the Bible? When we come to the last two chapters of the bible, we do not find religion, morality, ethics or edification. But we see a city, New Jerusalem. Many Christians think that the New Jerusalem is a heavenly mansion. This is a distorted view of biblical eschatology. Whilst most Christians are eager to go to heaven, God's desire is to come down from heaven for an expression on the earth. Essentially, I am not discounting completely the heaven theology but the truth is, that going to heaven should not be the ultimate nor a burning urgent priority of a believer. The revelation of scripture is to show us that we are bringing heaven here. Rev 21:2, *"And I John saw the holy city,* **new Jerusalem, coming down from God out of heaven**, *prepared as a bride adorned for her husband"*. The New Jerusalem is the ultimate consummation of God's working in both in the old and in the new creation. This is the conclusion of the bible, the New Jerusalem as God's eternal habitation. This is a revolutionising and transformative revelation. This is beyond the cross message but the glorious gospel of Christ. What is God's building? God's building is to dispense or impart Himself into us and work Himself into our being. **We need transformation more than the incidental "once off" born again Christian experience**. It is important to note that when we are born again John 3:3, *"Jesus answered and said unto him, Verily, verily, I say unto thee, Except a man be born again, he cannot see the Kingdom of God"*, John 1:12, *"But as many as received him, to them he gave power to become the sons of God, even to them that believe on his name"*, the God we receive is same to all believers but different experientially to individuals. The only begotten Son of God is unique and is for the declaration of God. In God's mind, it is for us to be an expression of Him.

In eternity future, Christ will not only be God but also man. He will not only be the Son of God, but also the Son of man. Since the word has been incarnated in the flesh, He is also a man, the Son of man with an uplifted humanity forever. After incarnation, He is still God but God and man. He is still the Son of God but the Son of man. In addition to being a Son of God, for eternity in future He will be the Son of man. In eternity past He was God, solely divine having no humanity. However, in eternity future, He will be God and man, the Son of God and the Son of man both divine and human having divinity as well as humanity. He will have two natures, two essences and two substances divinity and humanity. To us Jesus is the Son of God and to the devil, Satan, Jesus is the Son of man. The devil is not afraid of Jesus being the Son of God. He is afraid of Jesus being the Son of man. **This is unquestionable theological legal fact which the devil fears with trembling.**

A number of times when Jesus was casting demons out of people and demons addressed Him as the Son of God, Jesus silenced them (Mathew 8:29), Mark 3:11-12. He was acting as Son of man. When the devil tempted Jesus in the wilderness by saying, *"if you are the Son of God speak that these stones may become loaves of bread."* Matthew 4:3. He resisted the temptation as Son of man, Mathew 4:4 *"men shall not live by bread alone"*

Jesus maintained His standing being a Son of man. Satan is not afraid of the Son of God, he is afraid of the Son of man. Why is Satan afraid of man? Because in His economy, God had said that Satan must be defeated by man. God has no intention of dwelling in Himself. Divinity is not God's dwelling desire. God's intention in His economy is to dwell in humanity. Isaiah 66:1, *"Thus saith the Lord, The heaven is my throne, and the earth my footstool; where is the house that ye build unto me? And where is the place of my rest?"*

Obviously, there are number of contributing factors to that difference. We need to appreciate the two-sided view of the Word.

There is an objective side (normative) view and the subjective (experiential) side of God's word. The objective perspective is that which is factual and the positional. The subjective perspective is that which is experiential (existential), the practical. Therefore, there is the objective reality and subjective reality which we need to understand as we study the Bible. The Bible teaches about righteousness by faith in believing in our Lord Jesus Christ for sanctification.

II Corinthians 5:21, *"For he hath made him to be sin for us, who knew no sin; that we might be made the righteousness of God in him"*, 1 Corinthians 1:30, *"But of him are ye in Christ Jesus, who of God is made unto us wisdom, and righteousness and sanctification and redemption"*. We are made unto righteousness in Christ before the foundation of the world. This is objective or positional righteousness but then we need to be partakers of God's word as subjective side which is experiential. This produces the fruit of righteousness which basically come from right living – experiencing that upright living a life which reflects the person of Christ and His attributes. The exhibition of the fruit of the Spirit (Galatians 5:22, Matthew 23:17-19, John 17:17, 1Thessalonians 2:13 1 Peter 1:2),

According to Matthew 23:17 we see how the temple sanctified gold. It was the temple that made the gold holy. The gold in the market place although there was nothing sinful about it, was not holy until it had been offered to God and put into His holy temple. Only then was the gold sanctified Matthew 23:20. The Lord Jesus assert that the altar sanctified the sacrifice. It was not holy until it was offered to God on the altar. Just like on food it is sanctified by prayer 1 Timothy 4:4-5, *"For every creature of God is good, and nothing to be refused, if it be received with thanksgiving. For it is sanctified by the word of God and prayer*, but when it is in the market place it is common but when places on the saint's table it is sanctified by prayer. Application of all these verses gives a variety of definitions on a wide range of foundational biblical concepts. Sanctification, then would mean a change of position in Christ and therefore sanctification is a positional matter. This is a function of the Spirit of God after the resurrection and ascension of Christ. Precisely, focussing on the cross only will deprive a believer of the additional knowledge important to live victoriously in Christ. Our victory is not only in Christ Him crucified, but the resurrected, ascended, exalted, crowned King who descended as the Spirit on Pentecost. Glory to God as we now understand that beyond the cross, crucifixion, there is a lot to learn to strengthen our faith.

It could be unjust to conclude this chapter without mentioning the matter concerning holiness. This is sometimes considered as a very controversial and probably the most misunderstood **topic** in the Church today. **Question, is holiness sinless perfection? We believe according to biblical truth revealed in epistles. Sinless perfection is Not an accurate interpretation of HOLINESS.** However, holiness like sanctification is a positional as well as dispositional in nature. In addition, sanctification is not only a matter of changing our position but also changing for disposition. Sanctification is to work God's holiness into us by having God's divine nature imparted into our being. This is not only positional sanctification but dispositional sanctification which is a product of Christ as the life giving Spirit giving the grace to live right. This Spirit saturates all the inwards parts of our being with God's divine nature II Peter 1:3-4, *"According as his divine power hath given unto us all things that pertain unto life and godliness, through the knowledge of him that hath called us to glory and virtue: whereby are given unto us exceeding great and precious promises: that by these ye might be partakers of the divine nature, having escaped the corruption that is in the world through lust"*. This is to work God's holiness into our whole being. We may call this dispositional sanctification. It is important to detoxify ourselves from religious thinking with regards to biblical holiness and sanctification. However, it is important to remember that genuine holiness and sanctification is only achievable by the Spirit of GRACE. For believers, to know their position in Christ is key. We are not holy or sanctified because of our good behaviours but by believing in Jesus Christ through the Spirit of Grace.

Justification, holiness, sanctification, righteousness and perfection are essentially a product of the functioning of the Spirit of Christ in human spirit but largely linked to (Rom 12v2) the renewing of our minds. The thinking patterns of man determine his belief system. As wrong believing result in wrong behaviours. **However, we are not advocating for self-effort or behavioural modification but the Grace to practise and apply the Word of God. These aspects of redemption discussed are not a reality because of human effort**. Self-effort is more humanistic and frustrating but we need to rely on the Spirit of Grace who gives us the capacity to do His will. **"Phillipians 2:13 .....For it is God who works in you both to will and to do of his good pleasure"**

Thirteen

Christ in His Glory as the Great High Priest

The Bible is the book that defines the glory of Christ in the heavens after His resurrection and in His ascension. **Actually, the Bible is the documentary of the glory of God in Christ. It is the book of His glory.**

The book of Revelation in particular gives us a clear, divine picture of Christ in His **In Ascension** Revelation 1:13-16 we see the description of Christ on the throne in the third heavens. On verse 13 interesting to note, **"He is one like unto the Son of man, clothed with garment...."** He is the Son of man this settles the theological debate among various bible scholars on the corporeality of Christ in His ascension. Even Stephen in "(Acts 7:56)" saw Christ as the Son of Man. Furthermore, Matthew 26:64 shows us that He is the Son of man now sitting in the heavens and coming back in the future. Also Revelation tells us that He is the Son of Man among the local Churches and that He will return as the Son of Man Rev 14:14. Hence, I Timothy 2:5 written well after His ascension still call Him *"the Man Christ Jesus".* Our Saviour is a man who has the message and the mandate to discharge the purpose of God in the universe. Although, He is resurrected, Jesus is still a man, a resurrected man, an uplifted, immortalised and glorified man, a man who is in ascension; on the throne in the heavens. Jesus is qualified to be our Saviour because He is both God and man. This is why His salvation is *"so great salvation"* Hebrews 2:3. Great, not only in the element of God but also in the element of man. All the divine attributes and human virtues are integrated as the ingredients of the "so great a salvation". In this salvation man is transfused with divinity. This is the mystery of the new creation in Christ. New creation is highest demonstration of His wisdom and is incomparable. Even Satan with his craftiness cannot comprehend this height of divine ingenuity. The supernatural disposition of the new creation always confuses demons and strategically the regiments of the kingdom of darkness are always in disarray and panic. This is the reason as believers we are not supposed to fear demons. We are expected to command with authority.

Rev 1:13, *"...clothed with a garment down to the foot...."* In typology garments signify expression. This is especially true of the priestly garments that were for glory and beauty. Beauty and glory are both for expression. Hence, the priestly garments are the expression of Christ's human beauty and divine glory. The garments worn by the high priest were unusual. First, there was a tunic; which may have reached ankles. Over the tunic was a robe, which reached the feet and upon the robe there was the ephod. Upon the ephod there were the breastplate and the two shoulder pieces. All these garments contain significant aspects of typology regarding Christ with the church.

The Expression of God

Christ is the expression of God. The incarnate Christ is the embodiment of God and this embodiment is an expression. No one has ever seen God, but the Son of God, the only begotten was manifested in Him (John 1:18). This manifestation of God in Christ is God's expression. This means that Christ is the expression of the invisible and mysterious God. As expression of God, Christ makes the invisible God subjective. When we contact Christ we contact the practical and experiential God. The expression of God is both individual and corporate. As God's expression, Christ is not only individual but also corporate. When Christ was on earth he was the individual expression of God but after his death and resurrection, this expression became corporate. Christ is the centrality and universality of the essence of God. The theology behind the scripture in John 14:8-9 is fascinating. This was the discourse between Phillip and Jesus about the Fatherhood of God. Jesus said to Phillip, *"….he that seen me has seen the Father…."* and John 10:30 Jesus said, *"I and my Father are one"*. It appears to me that even when believers go to heaven they might possibly not even see God.but the crowned Christ the enthroned King. I am convinced the furtherest we might go is to see Christ the embodiment of God. I sincerely think the element which is central to our theology should be focussing on Christ, NO CHRIST, NO GOD. Christ is the distinction and demarcation from other faiths. Dr P.Kenos, a well–respected Theologian said, **'"Christ is the paragon of distinguishability, incomparability, ethereality, honourability, eviternity and eternality therefore He cannot be related to any other known faiths ."**

In Rev 1:13 we see Christ in a long garment worn by the High Priest in the Old Testament Isaiah 6:1, *"In the year that king Uzziah died I saw also the Lord sitting upon a throne, high and lifted up, and his train filled the temple"*. According to this verse, Isaiah had a vision of the Lord sitting in the temple. The word "train" here refers to the Lord's long robe. The prophet does not tell us how long this skirt was but he tells us that it filled the temple. No one has even seen a bride whose wedding garment so long that it filled the place where the wedding was held. No bride has such a fullness but this is related or equated to the Lord; who fills the temple, His dwelling place. That was a vision showing the expression of God. In this universe we know that all things consist in Him Colossians 1:17. Ephesians 1:23 says that the Church is the fullness of the one who fills all in all. How great is this Christ? He is all-inclusive and all-extensive, filling all in all. Scripture talks of the temple. Prophetically, this temple is the corporate Christ, the Church, the new creation which is the habitation of God. This is Christ we see in His ascension. In the book of Revelation actually, the ascension of Christ is one of the most fascinating and intriguing post-crucifixion phenomenon.

We need also to appreciate the significance of the various aspects of the priestly garments. We have to see the principle that all these garments are expression. They are signs, symbols and expression of Christ. This garment in typology signifies holiness and righteousness of God.

The High Priest and the Throne of Grace

Apart from the book of Revelation, the book of Hebrews supremely and outstandingly describes Christ in His ascension. We see in the book of Hebrews; Christ is seen as the Son of God, the Son of man, the captain of our salvation and the Great Apostle. All these qualifies Him to be our High Priest. Christ is our High Priest in the heavens and on the throne to minister God to us.

Hebrews 4:14, *"**Seeing then that we have a Great High priest, that is passed into the heavens,** Jesus the Son of God, let us hold fast our profession."*

We see the Lord Jesus firstly sent from God to us through incarnation (Hebrews 2:14) to be an Apostle (Hebrews 3:1), to lead us into glory and rest. He then went back from us to God through resurrection and ascension to be our High Priest to bear us in the presence of God. The very Christ we need and have today in the Sabbath rest of the Church life is our High Priest. The High Priest is supposed to be in the Holy of Holies. Interesting question, Where is Christ today? He is continually in the Holy of Holies. Our High Priest is not on the altar offering sacrifices nor in the Holy Place preparing showbread, lighting lamps and burning incense. He is in the Holy of Holies. Most Christians only have Christ who is on the altar that is Christ on the cross; the crucified one. Some Christians have Christ only in the Holy Place. The highest attainment in their spiritual seeking is that of a Christ preparing showbread, lighting the lamp and burning incense in the Holy Place. They have missed the High Priest in the Holy of Holies. The main function of the High Priest today is neither at the altar nor in the Holy place but in the Holy of Holies, where God's presence and Shekinah glory are. Yes, He was on the cross, but as Hebrews 1:13 reveals. His work on the cross has been finished and now He is sitting on the right hand of God in the heavens. No place is closer than this. This must be the place to crave for This is the place of victory and safety. The place we hear His voice from Psalms 18v 6 "...........*he heard my voice out of his temple .*"............. As we are His *corporate temple* His voice is heard from within us, in our human spirit which is intermingled with Spirit of Christ. This is the Holy of Holies, the Throne of Grace in the heavens.

According to the Old Testament, whenever the High Priest went to the presence of God in the Holy of Holies he bore upon His shoulders two onyx stones on which were engraved the names of the children of Israel. He also wore the breastplate in which the twelve previous stones engraved with the names of the children of Israel. This signified that the children of Israel were on the shoulder of and the breast of the High Priest. Since the shoulder signifies strength and the breast love, the people of God were safe with the High Priest. When the High Priest was in the Holy of Holies, when he was there all the people were with him. Likewise, when God looks at Christ our High Priest in the Holy of Holies, He sees us upon the shoulder and breast of Christ. This Christ our High Priest in the heavens bears us before God. Right now we are upon His shoulder and upon His breast in the Holy of Holies. We are there with Him in the Shekinah glory of God. **This is mystery of the Gospel, *Christ in us the hope of Glory.***

As Christ bears us before God in the Holy of Holies, He ministers God into our being. Therefore, in our endeavour to seek

God we should not be content to remain in the outer court nor staggering in the Holy Place but we should press on to the Holy of Holies where God's presence and the Shekinah glory are. This is only achieved through prayer, fellowship in the Word and our constant engagement with the Spirit in the Holy of Holies. The experience of Christ as our High Priest undoubtedly is in our human spirit and needs constant practise to mature in fellowship and be sensitive to His voice John 10 v27"........*My sheep hear my voice...*". Psalm 29 speaks of the *voice, the voice, the voice.* The emphasis here is on the voice. We need to constantly hear His voice. Rom 8 v 14. The leading in this verse speaks of the sensitivity in identifying His voice.

The Christ is the heavenly ladder, the Holy of Holies in the heavens is joined to our spirit. This wonderful Christ is both in the heavens and also in our spirit. This is a mystery which cannot be appreciated just with our intellectual cognitive abilities. **It is in the realm of His transcendence, eviterntiy and ethereality.** This is the mystery of Godliness that God was made manifest in the flesh. The incarnational principle. The ingenuity and splendiferous manifest wisdom of God, our God. Satan and his demons cannot get close to this level and yet the new creation redemptively has been elevated to this dimension. Amazing Grace this is the **SUPREMACY OF OUR GOD** above all other gods recorded in human history. This is the reason why as believers we should be bold in our position in Christ. The only possible strategy the Devil can employ to defeat believers is make sure that they remain in ignorant state with regards to who they are in Christ. Romans 8:34 says Christ is at the right hand of God interceding for us and Romans 8:10 *says that Christ is also within us.*

Our High Priest, Christ who is great in His Person, qualification work, accomplishment and attainment has passed through the heavens Hebrews 4:14 and stripped principalities and powers and made a public spectacle of them. Colossians 2:15, *"And having spoiled principalities and powers, he made a shew of them openly, triumphing over them in it".* Also this Christ, the High Priest as one who have been tried in all respects like us, he is able to sympathise with our weakness. Hebrews 4:15, *"For we have not an high priest which cannot be touched with the feeling of our infirmities; but was in all points tempted like as we are, yet without sin"*. After the unveiling of the High Priest we should also appreciate the fact that there is the throne of grace. **What is this throne of Grace?** To understand this we need revelation, which is, essentially, spiritual conceptualisation. With our natural mind this realm is unreacheable. 1 Cor 2v14"………. *the natural mind cannot receive the things of the Spirit……..for these are spiritually discerned."* Hebrews 4:16, *"…**come forward with boldness to the throne of grace….***"*This throne is a vastly extensive spirtual realm or domain which cannot be captured by our natural eyes. It is not a physical structure as our natural minds would want us to conceptualise or visualise. Our God does not have a physical throne like our natural leaders. The anthropomorphic expressions we use are just to help us connect to Him relationally but He is not physical John 4 v 24"…..**God is Spirit** ………."

However, the typological aspects we see in the study of the Mosaic tabernacle should help us appreciate this concept of the throne. Authority and mercy signified by the propitiation cover (the mercy seat) over the ark of testimony (Exodus 25:17-21) in the Holy of Holies (Hebrews 9:3,5) sprinkled with the blood of Christ (Leviticus 16:15) (Hebrews 9:12). It is here that God meets and commune with His people. When we come to the throne of grace through the blood, we meet with God and commune with Him. Fundamentally, this throne of Grace is subjectively operational in our human spirits. **This is the essence of His immanecy, corporeality and the principle of His universal accessibility**. Whaa, whaa, awesome truth.

God's Habitation in our Spirit

Hebrews 4:16 tells us to *"come forward with boldness to the throne of grace".* Since the throne of grace is in heaven, how can we come forward to it while we are still on earth? The theological understanding of this scripture is the revelation of the Christ who is sitting on the throne of grace in heaven who is also now in us, that is in our spirit. 2 Timothy 4:22, Romans 8:10,34. We are now the habitation of God through the spirit Ephesians 2:22. As Christ is in our Spirit, both the Father and the Spirit are also in our spirit John 14:20,23, Romans 8:16. The Triune God is in our spirit. This is the reality of our redemption in Christ. This is the truth which Professor W.R. Cains called, **The Ascended and Dimensionless Truth.** At Bethel the house of God the habitation of God, which is the gate of heaven, Christ is the ladder who joins earth to heaven and bring heaven to earth (Genesis 28:12-17, John 1:51). Although the throne of grace is in heaven, our wonderful Christ has brought the third heaven into our spirit the very place when God's habitation on earth is today.

Our spirit may be called today's Bethel. Coming boldly to the throne of grace is therefore a matter of our spirit. If we are in the unrenewed mind it is difficult to enter the Holy of Holies. The mind has to be decongested of the stuffy and worldly mindset Rom 12:1-2". ......*be transformed by the renewing of your mind.* If we are soulish persons staggering in the wilderness of our soul we shall be far away from the Holy of Holies. The spirit is the place of God's habitation today, it is the gate of heaven where Christ is the ladder that joins us the people on earth to heaven and brings heaven to us. Whenever we turn to our spirit we enter into the gate of heaven and touch the throne of Grace in heaven through Christ as the heavenly ladder. This is where the concept of prayer and worship come into play. The Spirit of God actually operate transformatively in this environment. Also the Word has to be the spiritual catalyst for supernatural manifestations. For the word of God pierce into the depths of our being and separate our spirit from our wandering mind (Hebrews 4:12). As long as we are in our spirit we have the gate of heaven. Within the gate is the throne of grace. It should not take time to enter the Holy of Holies because there is no distance between it and our spirit. The Spirit brings His immanecy into reality.

We should therefore be able to have this vision of Christ in ascension and.being always in partnership with the Holy Spirit. The truth is Jesus cares for His people, He intercedes for saints to the Father, He prepares a table before our enemies, He causes us to triumph, He answers prayers, He is the faithful burden bearer. We are born of Him and victory is our portion. *Glory to God!*

If as believers, we have a clear understanding of the priesthood of Christ our prayer lives should be completely transformed. Prayer, then should not be an excessive agonising and self-punishing labour, it is an understanding that our prayers are essentially an expression of our faith through Christ the High Priest who is objectively in the Holy of Holies in the heavens and also experientially indwelling in us. GLORY to God in the highest. **Our GOD REIGNS SUPREME IN WISDOM, POWER AND GLORY.**

Fourteen

Christ the High Priest in the Order of Melchizedek

1 Peter 2:5, *"Ye also, as lively stones, are built up a spiritual house, a holy priesthood, to offer up spiritual sacrifices, acceptable to God by Jesus Christ."*

1 Peter 2:9, *"But ye are a chosen generation, a royal priesthood, a holy nation, a peculiar people; that ye should shew forth the praises of him who hath called you out of darkness into his marvellous light".*

Revelation1:6, *"And hath made us kings and priests unto God and his Father; to him be glory and dominion for ever and ever, Amen".*

It is abundantly clear in scriptures that the idea of priesthood has been in the mind of God from eternity past. The tabernacle to function in accordance with God's standard priesthood has to be introduced. In the previous chapter I talked about the High Priesthood of Christ in His ascension. But now I am impressed to touch this priesthood in relation to Melchizedek one of most intriguing characters recorded in the bible as first mentioned in the book of Genesis. This is Melchizedek King of Salem. How does this intriguing biblical character connect or relate to Christ? We see the bible describing Christ as the High Priest in the order of Melchizedek. We need to understand according to the old system there was the order of Aaron, and also of Christ, according to the order of Melchizedek.

We understand Aaron did not like honour unto himself but

was called and established by God to be the High Priest Hebrews 5:4; verse 1. This is true of Christ. He did not glorify Himself to become a High Priest, He was ordained by God in His resurrection according to the order of Melchizedek (Hebrews 5:5-6) verse 6, *"…Thou art a priest forever after the order of Melchizedek…."* Also in Psalms 110:1-4, *"The Lord said unto my Lord, sit thou at my right hand, until I make thine …….. The Lord hath sworn, and will not repent, Thou art a priest for ever after the order of Melchizedek".* This refers to Christ in His ascension and enthronement which in addition to His resurrection are further qualifications for Him to be our High Priest. It is important to note that Christ was not only resurrected from among the dead, but He ascended to the height of the universe. As mentioned previously that Christ overcame the gravitation of the earth, overcoming the frustrating attack of the demons on the earth. When he entered the air as Colossians 2:15 reveals; He stripped off the principalities and powers and made a show of them openly.

The interesting spiritual practical reality is that in His ascension the entire humanity was in His glorified temple which later descended as the Holy Ghost on the day of Pentecost. "His ascension unmasked, paralysed and permanently immobilised the demonic world" **Dr. Kenty Hoffman said in his Thesis the Lordship of Christ.** After His ascension He is now sitting on the right hand of God in the heavens and our spiritual position is that we are seated with Him Ephesians 2:6, *"And hath raised us up together, and made us sit together in heavenly places in Christ Jesus".* This is the eternal security we have in Him. Colossians 3:3 *"…. We are hid with Christ in God".* In actuality, we are with Him in glory. As believers the glory in Christ is our habitation. ***His glory marks that inseparability between the redeemed and Christ.***

<u>The Ascended Christ a Priest like Melchizedek</u>

According to the Bible, there are only two orders of the priesthood, that in the order of Aaron and that in the order of Melchizedek. The priesthood of Melchizedek came from the eternal purpose of God. We do not know where Melchizedek came from. From the Biblical record he had no parents, no genealogy, no beginning of days nor end of life (Hebrews 7:1-3). This is the reason he signified Christ in his priesthood. Christ has no beginning nor end. Micah 5:2, *"... whose goings forth have been from old from everlasting"* this speaks of Christ. Hebrews 1:12, *"....thou art the same and thy years shall not end".* Christ the embodiment of eternity and the deity of the Godhead. The priesthood of Christ in the order of Melchizedek is the source of the new nativity and genealogy of the new creation. This is the reason why the subject of generational curses becomes a controversial discourse among believers today. **Here is question?** *If a new creation, the regenerated man is in Christ, how then can generational curses become a subject of concern?* Theological debate has been raised on this subject.

My personal view is that, there is no connection between new creation and generational curses because nativity would have changed. Therefore, spiritually I believe there is a distinct disconnect Jeremiah 31v29".......*the fathers have eaten a sour grape, and the children's teeth are set on edge".* If the fathers have transgressed the blame should not be levelled against the children. That spiritual disconnect must be appreciated. Why should the curses rest upon the children especially if the children are a new creation in Christ. 2 Corinthians 5 v17 becomes a reality, a new living entity which has never been in existence comes into being. The entry of the Spirit of regeneration in man should be the opening of a new life span in that life. Essentially, divinity overshadows humanity as we believe in Jesus Christ. This reminds us again on the new creation paradigm.

Also of interest to note is that Melchizedek when he met Abraham, (Genesis 14:18-20) he did not come to Abraham to receive tithes from him, but to minister to him the bread and wine. One night, before He left His disciples the Lord Jesus ministered to them the bread and wine (Mathew 26:26-27). What is the significance of the bread and wine used on the Lord's table? The Lord Himself said of the bread, *"this is my Body"* Matthew 26:26 and of the wine this is my blood (verse 28). This indicates that the bread and wine on the table signify the **"processed God"** portraying the Christ who is the embodiment of God, has been processed that he might be ministered unto us.

Christ as the High Priest in this order of priesthood is ministering life and peace to humanity. Therefore, the priesthood in the order of Melchizedek is the priesthood of life and peace. It is the priesthood of building lives to fulfil God's eternal purpose of the earth. This is the reason why the New Testament ministers are supposed to minister life through the Spirit not death. They are supposed to preach new covenant of life not the old dead covenant of death. *"....For the letter killeth but the Spirit giveth life"* actually Christ Himself is now the Spirit, the life giving Spirit 1 Corinthians 15:45. The building Spirit which is building this massive "organic and spiritual infrastructure" called the Church, the body of Christ, the *"ekkelesia"* of God, the habitation of God on the earth, the moving, organic temple, the living tabernacle which is not built with the hands of man but by the Spirit of resurrection.

Melchizedek although he was a King, he did not come as a king but the priest of the Most High God coming to Abraham with bread and wine. This seems simple and rather unexciting, but it is profound. In the bible bread denotes the life supply. The Lord Jesus said, *"I am the bread of life"* John 6:35 meaning that He is the bread from heaven which gives us life. In the bible wine signified the blood which accomplishes redemption in order to quench our thirst. As fallen people we were under God's condemnation. The Lord Jesus chose wine to signify His redeeming blood saying, *"drink ye all of it; for this is my blood of the New Testament which is shed for many for the remission of sins"* (Matthew 27:28). Melchizedek's coming is to minister bread and wine to Abraham, the father of the called race, signified Christ's coming to minister Himself as God to us.

Fundamentally, what is supremely important is the understanding that the high priesthood of Christ brought in the termination of the old Mosaic covenant so that there might come into being a new nation, a people in the new covenant relationship with God and out of this covenant people should come to the redeemer of the creation. The old priesthood of Aaron which was largely anchored on sacrifices of blood and animals in the temple was terminated. All the offerings, ceremonies, laws, regulations and holy days as explained in the book of Leviticus were obliterated and rendered obsolete. Hebrews 8:13, *"In that he saith, A new covenant, he hath made the first old. Now that which decayeth and waxeth old is ready to vanish away".*

Therefore, it is important to realise that there must be a clear-cut distinction in the mind of the Church between the Mosaic covenant and the new covenant in the blood of Christ. Jesus was the fulfilment of the Abrahamic covenant, hence the Mosaic law automatically became dysfunctional.and oboselete.

The new creation introduced to people a new law that Jesus gave in John 13:34-35, *"A new commandment I give unto you, that ye love one another; as I have loved you, that ye also love one another. By this shall all men know that ye are my disciples, if ye have love one another".* This law is to govern this new creation, the new covenant people. Actually, Hebrews 8:1-2 tells us that Jesus is the high priest of the new covenant people. When the veil of the temple was torn in two from top to bottom as recorded in Matthew 27:50-51, it was the end of the earthly Holy of Holies. It no longer functions. The new holy of holies is in heaven, Jesus is our High Priest. 1 Peter 2:1-9 tells us of the two priesthoods on earth now, the priesthood that offers up sacrifices of worship and love and royal priesthood that shows forth the excellence of Him who called us out of darkness into light (Colossians 1:13). Through this priesthood of the ascended Christ is not only for the forgiveness of sins but of eternal life and a new creation.

According to the book of Hebrews Christ offered Himself as the unique sacrifice for sin and solved the problem of sin once and for all. Then in His ascension He brought His blood into the Holy of Holies in the heavens and sprinkled it in the presence of God, thereby accomplishing redemption. Now as far as redemption is concerned, it is a fait accompli, a done deal. Christ has nothing to do with it. He is sitting on the right hand of God. However, He still needs to be our High Priest not to go to God but to come to us. He does not come to us to deal with sins but to minister the bread and wine which signify Himself, who, for our supply and satisfaction was processed through death and resurrection. This surpasses redemption.

On the subject of the blood of redemption, I think it is important to highlight or clarify one noted distortion and misconception among the saints. The blood actually is not "liquid substance" which Christ took to the heavenly Holy of Holies, but the 'blood sprinkled' is a metaphoric term. I strongly believe that the blood is the Eternal Spirit, *"....through the eternal spirit offered himself without spot to God...."* Hebrews 9:14.

The Ascended Christ and Sabbath Rest

I am impressed to comment briefly on the subject of the Sabbath day. We have a number of brothers who believe on the importance of observing a day as part of their worship. Which from hermeneutics, biblical interpretation standpoint it is a distortion. ***What is the correct scriptural interpretation of Sabbath?*** Sabbath is not merely a rest after a completion of work but it means satisfaction. If your desire has not been satisfied you cannot have rest. The best rest; the real rest is the satisfaction of our heart's desire. In consideration of God's desire from eternity past to the present we see that God's eternal plan is to have Himself expressed and represented by man. It was for this reason He created man in His own image and gave him dominion over all things (Genesis 1:26). When man is on the earth expressing God and representing Him; God's desire is satisfied. When we are satisfied in our God's desire we are resting even as we are labouring and working. When the Bible first mentions man it speaks of God's image and dominion, indicating man was destined to express God with His dominion. In other words man has been ordained by God to express him and represent Him to His creation in the earth.

When we come to the end of Bible after centuries of God's work of creation, redemption, transformation and glorification we see the city with God's appearances. God in Christ, sitting upon the throne has the appearance of Jasper (Revelation 4:2-3) and the entire city of New Jerusalem also has appearance of Jasper (Revelation 21:11) signifying that God is fully expressed through that city. Therefore, in eternity future will be fully expressed in New Jerusalem. That will be the true Sabbath rest to God. So the true meaning of Sabbath is rest, God's desire fully satisfied. Christ is our rest and fulfilment of God's rest. Christ is the embodiment of Sabbath not a day.

God's economy is dynamic, always developing. We see Jesus; the second man after Adam baptised in water; God was happy and satisfied, saying **"This is my beloved Son in whom I am well pleased"** Matthew 3:17. We see God satisfied in the Lord Jesus, so God's satisfaction His Sabbath. This is the correct biblical interpretation of Sabbath.

Also the church; the enlargement of Christ is God's Sabbath. The church is the enlargement and the expression of Christ. If Christ was God's Sabbath then how much more extensive should the Church be as His Sabbath? If Israel was God's rest, Sabbath, then how much more should the Church be? *The Church is the new man with qualities of immortality and eviternality* (Ephesians 2:15; 4:24). If God enjoyed a Sabbath rest after the creation of the old man, He must have a greater rest after the creation of the new man. We are not in the age of the creation of the old man but the age of the new man. God has a new Sabbath because He has secured a new man to express and represent Him. According to the principle established by the first mention of Sabbath rest after the creation of man; there must be a new and better Sabbath after the creation of the new man. We are in this new Sabbath today. So the real Sabbath according to the philosophy of God's divine plan and purpose is not a day but satisfaction of His desire. He obtained His habitation by Christ's completion of all the redemptive processes. In Matthew 12:8 he said that He was the **'Lord of the Sabbath'.**

More emphatically we see in the epistles in the book Colossians 2 v 16 *Let no man judge you in meat, or drink or in respect of an holyday, or of new moon or Sabbath days"*. The Amplified Bible says, "Do not be overthrown by vain philosophies and doctrines." Keeping the Sabbath day is no longer relevant because Jesus, with new priesthood abolished the law, Sabbaths and sacrifices which were more pronounced by the old order, the old covenant. It is no longer in a day but in our relationship with Christ the Spirit. Christ our High Priest is our rest daily. Our Sabbath which we need to live in and rest in Christ by faith. For grace is manifested in this way.

Fifteen

The Ascended Christ as our Heavenly Minister

We have an interesting picture of our heavenly Christ a High Priest sitting on the throne of the majesty in the heavens.

Hebrews 8:1 says that we have a *"High Priest who sat down on the right hand of the throne of the majesty in the heavens"*. This is the heavenly Christ; the kingly and divine High Priest; our today's Melchizedek. Our High Priest today is not standing on the earth to accomplish redemption, He is sitting on the throne of the majesty in the heavens in glory and is leading many those who believe into glory. In glory in the majesty of the Godhead in the heavens and He is interceding restfully for the perfecting of His redeemed ones. This is not the work of the Aaronic priesthood but the ministry of the kingly and divine priesthood. Christ is not our Aaron standing on the earth but our Melchizedek sitting in the heavens, even on the throne of God with the divine majesty.

Christ is ministering in the true tabernacle in heaven joined to our spirit. In searching through scriptures I have discovered that in God's economy three things are always combined; the tabernacle or the sanctuary, the priesthood and the law. These three things which are one are combined for the fulfilment of God's economy. During the Old Testament, no one could separate these three things from each other. It is the same today. We have the sanctuary which is both in heaven and in our spirit, the priesthood and the better law of life. The sanctuary; priesthood and law that we enjoy today are much better than the old sanctuary, priesthood and the law. These old things were merely a shadow. These new items, which we are enjoying today are the reality of the shadow.

Hebrews 8:2 says that Christ is *"minister of the holy places even of the true tabernacle which the Lord pitch not man"*. Christ ministers in the true tabernacle in heavens, Christ brings us into the heavenly realm; from the earthly court into the heavenly ladder (Genesis 28:12) (John 1:51). The priests on earth served as the shadow (Hebrews 8:5) but the minister in heaven serves as the reality. His more excellent ministry in heaven serves the reality of the heavenly things in the divine dispensation. Precisely, Christ has a more excellent ministry. As a mediator of a better covenant enacted upon better promises. In this priesthood today we have a mediator; a man who goes between God and us. The mediator who is also the executor, the one who executes the will, the testament, the Christ, as the mediator is the executor in resurrection of the new covenant, the New Testament, which He bequeathed to us by His death. Therefore, we need to pursue for the revelation concerning our bequests in the new covenant.

The covenant which was enacted for us and bequeathed to us as the New Testament by Christ is a better covenant. Not only has this better covenant been enacted upon better promises of a better law; the inner law of life. Hebrews 8:10-12, *"For this is the covenant that I will make with the house of Israel after those days, saith the Lord; I will put my laws into their mind, and write them in their hearts: and I will be to them a God, and they shall be to me a people. And they shall not teach every man his brother, saying, know the Lord: for all shall know me, from the least to the greatest. For I will be merciful to their unrighteousness, and their sins and their iniquities will I remember no more"* but it was consummated with Christ's better sacrifice which have been accomplished for our eternal redemption and with the better blood of Christ which purifies our conscience (Hebrews 9:14). As the high priest of this better covenant Christ; the eternal Son of the living God, ministers with more excellent ministry (Hebrews 8:6) in the greater and more perfect tabernacle.

We have a better covenant which operates on better promises. These better promises which are given in Jeremiah 31:31-34, *"Behold, the days come, saith the Lord, that I will make a new covenant with the house of Israel, and with the house of Judah; Not according to the covenant that I made with their fathers in the day that I took them by the hand to bring them out of the land of Egypt; which my covenant they brake, although I was an husband unto them, saith the Lord: But this shall be the covenant that I will make with the house of Israel; After those days, saith the Lord, I will put my law in their inward parts, and write it in their hearts; and will be their God, and they shall be my people. And they shall teach no more every man his neighbour, and every man his brother, saying, Know the Lord; for they shall all know me, from the least of them unto the greatest of them"* Cross-scripturally quoted in (Hebrews 8:8-12) are two things; the forgiveness of sins and the law life. Under the old covenant there was no forgiveness of sins; only the covering of sins. In the new covenant we do not have just the covering of sins but the forgiveness of sins. In the new covenant today we also have the law of life not the law of letters.

Christ is carrying out the better covenant by making the legal facts in the new covenant effective as our heavenly minister with a more excellent ministry. Christ carries out the better covenant. Christ; *the heavenly minister,* executes the bequests in the New Testament. Whatever is a fact in the covenant is a bequest in the new testament. It is also important to note the difference between bequests and a fact. Facts refer to certain things that have been accomplished but not yet designated until bequeathed. After the accomplished facts have been bequeathed, they immediately become bequests designated for us. This is the difference between covenant and a testament, whatever is a covenant, is a fact; but whatever is in a testament is a bequest. Whatever were facts in the covenant have now become legally designated for us bequests in new covenant which have all become bequests in the will in the New Testament. There are four facts of the new covenant which have all become bequests in the New Testament; the propitiation for unrighteousness and for forgiveness of sins. *The imparting of the law of life, the blessing of having God and of being His people and the inward ability to know God.* **Knowing God is the quiantiessential** aspect of appropriating the benefits of the New Testament covenant. The basis of the new covenant is our understanding of the eternal purpose of God. God's divine intention is to dispense Himself into us and to work Himself into us as our life and everything until eventually He and we are mingled together and we become His expression to the whole universe. In this process, divinity is brought into humanity and humanity is mingled with divinity. God is God but He became man. We are men but we have God's life and nature.

As Christ is in the heavens, declared as the Firstborn Son through resurrection **He is appointed heir of all things.** Hebrews 1:2, *"Hath in these last days spoken unto us by his Son, whom he hath appointed heir of all things, by whom also he made the worlds"* and also Colossians 1:16 says that all things were created by and for the Son. John 13:3 tells us that the Father has given all things to the Son. The Son is Lord of all (Acts 10:36). He was inaugurated as the Lord of all into His office at the time of His ascension and anointed by God, but in His exaltation He was inaugurated as both the Lord and Christ to administrate God's operations and was designated as the legal Heir to inherit all things in God's economy.

In order to realise that we are the heirs of salvation we must be aware that God's economy has the Firstborn Son and many sons. The New Testament reveals that through Christ's death and resurrection the many sons of God were born (1 Peter 1:3). In God's salvation we are not only born of God to be His sons (John 1:12-13) but also made us **"heirs of God and joint-heirs of Christ"** (Romans 8:17, Galatians 4:7 and Titus 3:7). However with all these references it is also important to note that to be born as sons of God is one thing; to be made heirs of God is another thing. **Do you know the difference between an heir and a son?** You might be a son but not an heir. To be a son you are born but to be an heir, it requires maturity which is a product of a process of life. None of us can escape the processes demanded to maturity. Jesus Himself in His humanity could not circumvent the processes to elevation. It has to be constantly borne in our minds that there is nothing in life as microwave phenomena to success or heirship. The Bible records that Jesus (Hebrews 5:8)".........*yet He learned obedience by the things He suffered..."* In Chapter 12 the Bible records that Jesus *endured the cross. He had to go through. The Psalmists says even if I go through the valley ....Interesting to note also is that MATURITY is related to foresight. DR Raymond Stephens says,.........Failure to grow into maturity is the effect of lack of INSIGHT, insight essentially is REVELATION.* Before a boy becomes an heir, he has to mature. The purpose of God therefore is not only to have sons but to have sons who are matured to be joint-heirs requires maturity. **As Christ was appointed heir we are legally and spiritually joint-heirs, implying that we are partners in administering God's economy.** We are partners sharing the same interest in the divine corporation; Christ and the Church. As many sons who are the joint-heirs of Christ and His partners, compose the house of God, Bethel we are sons in the house of God. Hebrew 2:6 tells us that we are the sons of God. Then Hebrews 3:6 says that we are the house of God. This house is living because it is built with us the living sons of the living God. It is a matter of God being the Spirit and the indwelling Spirit. The living God is the Spirit that dwells in our regenerated Spirit. He is the house of God on earth. Hence, it is the habitation of God in our spirit. Ephesians 2:22, *"In whom ye also are builded together for a habitation of God through the Spirit".* We are the house of God composed of many sons with Christ, the Firstborn Son of God as the heavenly ladder. Therefore the church is the gate of heaven and bringing heaven to earth upon the ladder the angels are ministering as they ascend and descend.

The consciousness of the revelation of the ascended Christ particularly His ministry in the New Testament and His divine priesthood makes our position firm and unshakeable. It is a legal scriptural fact and a New Testament reality that we are not alone in this journey to accomplish God's will and His purpose on the earth. The consciousness of our joint heir-ship and partnership with Christ makes even intercession easier. We are joined with Him, 1 Corinthians 6:17, *"But he that joined unto the Lord is one Spirit".* The reality of the intermingling of divinity and our humanity. Having gone through the priesthood Christ in His ascension and His heavenly ministry it has dawned in my heart that as believers we sometimes do not live in the revelation about where we are and who we are in Christ. In view of Christ's redemptive accomplishments actually the devil has capitalised on the level of ignorance, passivity and naivety among believers. It is clear in my spirit that the message on our joint heir-ship is rarely preached. Surely we are joint-heirs with Christ. So be therefore conscious of this divine reality. The understanding of this revelation undoubtedly brings the spiritual laws in the New Covenant into effect.

I am reminded of the story in the Bible about the young king Josiah (II Kings 22:1-11). Read this passage we have limited space to quote it all. On verse 8 a book was handed over to him by the priest, Hilkiah, who later gave it to the scribe, Shaphan. Shaphan the scribe delivered the book to the king. On verse 11; the King rent his clothes and wept after reading the book. Why did the King weep and rent his clothes? My conclusion is that the King probably wept because of what he discovered in the book either about the law of God in relation to the nations of Israel, or probably about his Kingly mandate and privileges in relation to the kingdom of God. He was possibly operating on a level far below his position as the King. The position which was prophesied in the book of the law years back during the reign of King Manasseh. The King would not stand the power of discovery or revelation about himself. Strength and power to overcome your life challenges is concealed in the unknown realm. Actually, glory is in the unknown. Romans 8:26, *"....we know not....."* This is a reason revelation is the power behind God's word.

Revelation brings self-discovery, self-introspection, "self-audit" and self-repositioning. From this simple analysis I believe that greater portion of the challenges we sometimes encounter as believers originate from knowledge deficiency.

Our Lord Jesus said in John 8:32, *".....you shall know the truth ....."* Proverbs 24:5, *"....knowledge increases strength".* Dr Macbeth Marcus a renowned theologian said, **"The increase of knowledge is the gateway to deliverance".** We also see Jesus in John 11 on the raising of Lazarus. Verse 35 *"Jesus wept".* Why did Jesus weep? And yet, He is the embodiment of the omnipotent, omniscient and omnipresent God. The metabiological man who is the epitome of knowledge. He needed no introduction to the matrix in His creation. In weeping Jesus as a man with human feelings, was, empathetic and sympathetic to the loss of life or probably the realisation of the pain death is inflicting on humanity, the sting of death 1 Cor 15 v 55 & 56. The redemptive agenda became a living reality to Him. Possibly, the urgency on His divine assignment was intensified. His resolve to battle got stronger as the vision of the cross got amplified.and became more real. Another assumption here could be that Jesus was touched with the intensity of darkness among His people, Israel, the notable spiritual blindness. The ignorance among His people with regards to the economy of God. Probably, He realised the task ahead of Him because he knew that Lazarus was to be raised from the dead for the testimony to the unbelieving Jewish community. But the physiological fact was that Lazarus was now in a decomposed state. This needed another dimension of prayer so He wept as he was groaning in the Spirit. Another school of thought on the weeping of Christ could be probably the disturbing revelation of the level of unbelief among the people of God. Disbelieving God is tantamount to declaring indirectly that God, the Creator of universe and mankind can be a liar. The sum total of all these assumptions grieved Him, remember, also that the incarnate Jesus was one hundred percent man (**humanity**) and one hundred percent God (**divinity**). *In actuality His divinity spontaneously quickened*

His humanity to the realities around His spiritual environment. The historical narrative we all know Lazarus was raised from the dead ....
BY FAITH TO THE AMAZEMENT OF ALL AND MANY.

I have come to the realisation that our Christian walk is an adventure in endeavouring to discover the "unknown" about ourselves concerning our destiny. We need therefore to yield to the Spirit to lead us to the wealthy place. A place of destiny and revelation of the future. Psalms 66:12, *" : but thou broughtest us out unto a wealthy place".* I am reminded of Isaiah 45:3, *"And I will give thee the* **treasures of darkness,** *and hidden riches of* **secret places,** *that thou mayest know that I the Lord, which call thee by thy name, am the God of Israel".* This scripture used to confuse me. How could God give me treasures in "darkness"? I later realised that the word darkness, impliies, **the place you do not know.** It might not necessarily mean darkness from the perspective of the evil world of Satan. There is treasure in the unknown realm which you have not journeyed into. God wants us to partner closely with the Holy Spirit to reveal the hidden treasure deposited in us through Christ II Corinthians 4:7, *"but we have this treasure in the earthen vessels...."* He who has begun a good work in you will bring it to completion, Philippians 1:6. The discovery of knowing who you are in Christ is your position of strength. The philosophy of the new creation is underpinned on one major principle. The principle of transformation which is undergirded on the physchology of the renewal of the mind**, *the paradigmic shift which brings alignment to perspectives.***

GLORY TO GOD IN THE HIGHEST TO HIM BE ALL THE GLORY.

Sixteen

Christ the Great Apostle and the High Priest of our Confession

Hebrews 3:1, *"Wherefore, holy brethren, partakers of the heavenly calling, consider the **Apostle** and **High Priest** of our **Confession,** Christ Jesus:"*

Hebrews 10:23, *"Let us hold fast the profession of our faith without wavering: (for he is faithful that promised:)"*

One of the most striking characteristic feature of the ascended Christ is His infinite superiority over all prophets including Moses whom God used mightly to deliver Israel from the Egyptian bondage and Pharaohic tyranny. Christ is highly exalted above angels, prophets, Moses and any other earthly gods. Though the Jewish religion boast of Moses as their outstanding leader. Christ is also above all earthly priesthood, the Aaronic and all the Levitical priesthood. Christ is the High Priest superior to Aaron and Great Apostle superior to Moses. As an apostle, He was typified by Moses, as a High Priest, He was typified by Aaron. The Apostle is one who was sent to us from God and with God (John 6:46). The High Priest was the one who went to God with us (Ephesians 2:6). As the Apostle Christ came to share God with us that we might partake of His divine life, nature and fullness. As a High Priest, Christ went to God with us to present us to God that we and all our case might be fully cared for by Him. As an Apostle He was typified by Moses who came from God to serve the house of God (Hebrews 3:2-6). Though most people talk of Christ's High Priesthood, very few believers are familiar with His apostolic mantle. In fact, Christ is the first Apostle in the New Testament.

We need to examine again Hebrews 3:1 *"Consider the Apostle and High Priest of our confession, Jesus…."* This is a very interesting scripture displaying the heavenly universalistic and administrative position of the ascended Christ. Christ has a uniquely established function; to oversee and administer our confession. This is the reason Christianity is called **"The Great Confession"** Hebrew 4:14, *"Seeing then that we have a Great High priest, that is passed into the heavens, Jesus the Son of God, let us hold fast our profession."* Confession has a central role or function in affecting the realm of the spirit. The spiritual realities are brought into manifestation by the power of words, whether negative or positive the <u>governing law of confession</u> is applicable. Proverbs 18:21, *"Death and life are in the power of the tongue."*

Revelation and realisation only follow our confession. The word becomes practical only as we confess its reality. What you confess becomes a reality in your spirit. What is the meaning of the word confession? Confession comes from the Greek word *"Homologous"* meaning saying the same thing over and over again for the purpose of establishing the reality of a thing. Taking from the historical account of Jesus' life in the Gospels, we see Jesus walked in the light of His confession. He was the embodiment of what He confessed. E.W. Kenyon says, **"It is strange to note that faith follows in the footprints of our confession"** Dr Kames Mood, a reowned theologian added another perspective by stating that, **Confession is an important doctrinal aspect in Christianity but it is in the paediatrics of faith. Confession is entry level to faith but possession is maturity and maturity is aasociated with the sons of God.** After a careful consideration of this statement I came to the realisation that a believer cannot rise above his or her confession to possess the inheritance in Christ. You are, in actuality, a product of your confession as much as you're a product of redemption in Christ.

Psalms 107 *"Let the redeemed of the Lord say so...."* The Psalmist again says, *"Order my steps in thy word...."* 119:133. The word step here can be examined in the context of confession. Here the author is praying to God for Him to administer his steps (confession) so as to be firmly established in righteousness. There are a number of scriptural references with regard to confession, the power of the tongue and words all these are not within the scope of this edition. It is of paramount importance to guard our confessions.

The fact that Christ Himself as our High Priest and Apostle who watches over our confession shows that confession is not to be taken lightly. Professor Quest in his book **"Redemptive Realities"** says, ***"Confession management followed by possession is pivotal to our attainment of victory in Christ".*** I believe this is true, on the standpoint of confession. This is the reason apostle Paul in Hebrews 10:33 says, *"...Let us hold fast to the confession of our faith..."* Confession is the bedrock of your salvation and faith. Hold on it, have a tenacious spiritual grip to it. Desire to be an authentic testimony of Christ. Revelations 12:11, *"And they overcame him by the blood of the Lamb, and by the word of their testimony; and they loved not their lives unto the death."*

In reality, confession has its seat in the realm of the spirit. Both forces either the forces of darkness or forces of light would want to use our confession to establish a thing on the earth. Either good or evil. As a believer if you are persistently experiencing recurrent defeats in the hands of demons, check your ***"confession management pattern".*** Negative confession empowers demons. Demons are limited in knowledge and revelation so they wait to hear from what you say for them to build up an onslaught on your faith. The writer of the book of Job in chapter 22:28, *"Thou shalt also decree a thing, and it shall be established unto thee: and the light shall shine upon thy ways".* This scripture helps us understand this doctrine of confession. Essentially, confession is a law like the law of gravity it affects our lives whether we like or not. This is the main reason our Lord in His ascended position after crowned Lord of lords, and King of kings

Acts 10:36, *"...he is Lord of all"* immediately assumed an Apostolic and priestly oversight over our confession. Christ as the High Priest assumes the role of enforcing our confession as a spiritual principle or law which universally governs the establishment of a thing on earth. The truth is that the spiritual realm is more real than the physical. The physical reality is birthed by spiritual reality. Our confession becomes instrumental in the process of creation. Understanding of this law of confession brings us to the light of Matthew 16:19 where the theology of binding and loosening is derived from. The Lord here is saying to us, you have the spiritual authority to allow or disallow either in the positive or in the negative. I believe this probably could be the reason God had to mute Zacharias the priest in Luke1:20 ......***thou shall be dumb and able to speak until the days these things are performed***.............. God was concerned with His vision of the birth of John the Baptist for His economy. Any negative words would have caused the aborting of His vision and purpose. **GOD IS ALWAYS STRATEGICALLY PROPHETIC in His dealings with Man.** I am also strikingly impressed by the poetic and figurative expression by the prophet Isaiah in Chapter 28:18 he speaks of Israel's *"covenant with death"*. Essentially, this implies that your confession has the capacity to carry either death or life. The prophet uses the word covenant, agreement. We should not be in agreement or covenant relationship with any form of negativity for it is death and it capacitates demons to destroy your faith. It is important to note that by virtue of our fallen nature our bodies are not yet redeemed or glorified so we are always prone to gravitate towards negativity which orbits the dark world of Satan

Always be cognisant of the revelation of the 'trinity' of man. It is only the Spirit which has been redeemed by the regeneration. Our soul which is constituted by the will, emotion and mind has to go through the process of renewal (Romans 12:1-2). The body which is the externality is controlled by the inward parts, the spirit and soul. Essentially, understanding the background of this theology helps in managing confession. It is important to be focussed on the Word of

God. The Word of God shapes the trajectory for our faith journey. Knowledge and understanding. (Proverbs 4:7)

We have to be impressed by the truth that the entry of God in Christ on the earth was important not only to forgive sins but to herald the message of the Kingdom. Jesus Christ's main thrust in preaching the message of the Kingdom is essentially a capacity building agenda. The Kingdom is for the life and building. Capacity building is enhanced by our "confession management patterns". The indwelling Christ, the Great Apostle and High Priest of our confession enable us to subjectively experience the reality of our joint-heirship with Him. Isaiah 28:20, *"For the bed is shorter than that a man can stretch himself on it: and the covering narrower than that he can wrap himself in it."* This scripture gives us a clear picture of man in his fallen state. **The limitedness of the fallen humanity without Christ**. Like what Dr Kent Morrison said, ***"Without Christ in this life failure is an inevitable crisis"***, Colossians 2:10, ***"And ye are complete in Him…"*** In Him we are made perfect because He met all the requirements of God's legal and constitutional demands for redemption. Isaiah 53:10, *"Yet it pleased the Lord to bruise him…"* Matthew 17:5, *"…which said, this is my beloved Son, in whom I am WELL PLEASED…"* Our promotion, elevation, blessing, peace, justification and reconciliation is only through Christ. Christ is the pleasure of the Father and not the Mosaic Law, our hard work, observance of rules and regulations but faith in the redemptive work of Christ. Our minds have to be changed to always connect to the message of Grace. We need this revelation to stick. God is not really interested in us in our fallen state but Christ who is in us, His pleasure and treasure (Colossians 1:27). 2 Corinthians 4:7, *"But we have this treasure (Christ) in this earthen vessels…"* Christ is the desire of nations. Haggai 2:7, *"…. The desire of all nations shall come. This is Christ our High Priest in His ascended glory".* He is above the heavens of heavens and the heavens cannot contain Him. King Solomon in his prayer 2 Chron 6 v18 It is actually an interesting thought here about Christ and the heavens. In view of this thought the '**Heaven**

Theology' has to be revisited. Our focus as believers should be higher than heaven. Going to heaven should not be our obsession but Christ. Precisely, the, Heaven and the "Mansion Theology" in my view is a substandard goal for a believer. Therefore set the bar higher and lift up the standard, which, is Christ. Heaven is just a piece of His creation and He is the Creator. **So question?** Why should focus be placed on the creation than the Creator. Knowledge is an important base in building health confession patterns. In order to build faith, the Word is key but the word require a stirring from within which is normally achieved by confession. Also in a loss of confidence situations confession, that is saying the same thing over and over again, helps in regaining confidence. The walk of faith is not always an easy adventure, there is the need of focus and it is not easy to maintain faith in the midst of adversities. Therefore, by building a consistent confession patterns, focus, is maintained. In prayer, the quickest way to spiritual activation is confession of **HIS WORD.**

Seventeen

The Triumphant Christ and the Church

Romans 15:4, "For whatsoever things were written a foretime were written for our learning, that we through patience and comfort of the scriptures might have hope."

2 Chronicle 20:20-25 (Read the text we have limited space)

Here we have an interesting historical account of the children of Israel fighting against the Ammonites and Moabites as it had been always the case with Israel to always fight for what rightfully belonged to her. As it is the case with us too as believers, we are always confronted with the enemies of Christ in this faith adventure. As Apostle Paul encouraged the young evangelist Timothy in chapter 1Timothy 6:12, *"to fight a good fight of faith...."* I like what the scripture says, it is a good fight. Why a good fight? Good because the result is known, the winner is already declared beforehand that is why it is good. 2 Corinthians 2:14, *"Now thanks* be *unto God, which always causeth us to triumph in Christ..."* In Him we triumph and conquer. In Him victory is guaranteed as we set our minds on the finished work of Christ. Proverbs 21:31, *"The horse is prepared against the day of battle: but safety is of the LORD"* the word safety denotes victory, Christ is our victory.

We see here in 2 Chronicle 20, Judah defeats Ammon and Moab because of revelation. In our spiritual engagements, revelation is key to the manifestation of victory and His Glory. Christ through

His incarnation, crucifixion, resurrection and ascension brought victory to humanity. Christ restored dominion and authority for the church. Colossian 2:15, 2 Chronicles 20:25 then says, *".....they were three days in gathering the spoil, it was so much".* When the ascended Christ descended on the day of Pentecost, it was the beginning of the gathering of nations, the spoils, for Christ. A fulfilment of Psalms 1:8, *"....I shall give the heathen for thine inheritance and the uttermost parts of the earth for thy possession."* In Acts we see Christ, the Spirit, gathering the spoils for God's pleasure. The bringing of men to God and God to men was the delight of the heavenly Father.

It is always important to be conscious of our victory as we are on daily basis confronted with challenges in this life. We have to set our spiritual eyes on our Captain of our salvation (Hebrews 12:2), the Captain of our salvation, the ascended Christ. We wrestle from the position of victory. I like what Dr. Rossy Morrison says in his book. **"The Triumphant and Ascended Christ."** *"The arrival of a higher power in effect is the displacement and <u>obviation (removal)</u> of a lesser power".* Precisely, the lesser power has to bow in submission to the higher authority. The ascension, the crowning- glorification of Christ and His ultimate spiritual outburst on the day of Pentecost resulted in Christ occupying the entire "infrastructure" of the heavens and became universally recognisable and accessible. He occupies eternity and humanity as the living-giving Spirit. As He prophetically commanded in Luke 19:13, *".......Occupy till I come".* Christ wants the church to occupy its space with full realization of the joint heir-ship as spoken of in the Epistles of Apostle Paul. **On this basis therefore it makes biblical sense to disregard the overemphasis in the Church today on the heaven theology.** From this argument we see that God is deeply interested in believers in Christ having an **<u>occupation and dominating mindset on earth yet we see majority of believers have this "mediocre-evacuation" mindset which is escapistic in nature. Essentially, the work and glory is here on earth not in the heavens as always suggested by some retired, semi-retired, apostatic or novice believers.</u>** We are a triumphant community of believers, the general assembly of the church of Firstborn. We are His perfect representation in the earth. Therefore defeat in whatever form cannot be our portion.

Christ the Soon Coming King Our Blessed Assurance and Hope

Although Christians might not agree on all doctrinal details, there is no genuinely born again Christian who does not believe in the Second Coming of Christ. The Holy Spirit in us is the **blessed hope and assurance**. Known as the Spirit of Promise in the heavens, he is given as a pledge of our inheritance in Christ. **Why is the second coming of Christ also known as our blessed hope?** From the day that Jesus ascended into heaven, His followers lived with expectancy of His return. He told them He was coming back. They also believed He was coming back as we also believe that He is coming back. The coming of Christ is the most invaluable knowledge in possession of most Christians. This is in a way part of the source of our spiritual motivation, to continue holding on in spite of the obvious and fervent, insidious and subtle opposition from the Devil and his demons.

According to the Bible prophecy, we are living in the time between the comings, the first and the second coming of Jesus. Although the Old Testament prophets did not emphatically prophesy of His second coming as they were mandated to talk of the Messianic first coming and the Messianic age. There are a number of scriptural references which emphatically support the theological doctrine of His second coming. The one glorious Messianic age predicted by the Old Testament prophets unfolded in two different ages. This and the age to come. It is within the concept of the two ages that we find seeds of extreme theological tension which have caused innumerable eschatological, doctrinal distortions and gross misunderstanding. This tension has also triggered many debates, sometimes controversial, concerning the Kingdom of God. Is it a present reality or still a future hope? But we believe the Kingdom of God is a present reality though it will be fully manifested in the future.

Professor Hofferman, a renowned Theologian in Divinity says, "Eschatology is the language of the promise". This is undeniable truth; eschatology speaks of Christ and His future. I vehemently disagree with Dr Martin Koss in his thesis on eschatology. He claims that eschatology connected to Christology sound like an escapist theory or eschatology of defeat. No, I believe the eschatology of Christ is our blessed hope and we have abundant biblical supporting evidence on this theological position. Our Lord Jesus Christ is coming back. His coming back is not by vote or approval of man but it is and will be an act of God according to His eternal purpose.

We might have divergent views and hermeneutical differences in interpreting the methodological processes in His coming. But the truth is that He is coming back. Hebrews 10:37, *"For yet a little while, and he that shall come will come, and will not tarry."* **(Matthew** 24:33, Mark 13:28-32, Luke 21:29-33). The simple account of His Second Ascension in Acts 1:9-12. Verse 10-11, *"And while they looked stedfastly toward heaven as he went up, behold, two men stood by them in white apparel; which also said, Ye men of Galilee, why stand ye gazing up into heaven? This same Jesus, which is taken up from you into heaven, shall so come in like manner as ye have seen him go into heaven".*

Precisely, the theology of His second coming is not and cannot be a wishful thinking, a pathetic fallacy, nor can it be a fantastic dream of a handful of apocalyptic fanatics. Based on the biblical prophesies in scripture, the doctrine of His second coming cannot be a speculative doctrine. This is a reality for the restoration of all things. Of course, it cannot be denied. His coming back includes innumerable events which are beyond the scope of this book. Revelation 22:12, *"And behold I come quickly...."* I believe His coming will be the first of a train of tremendous events which is to make up the spectacular panorama of prophetic scripture.

Resurrection and Rapture

1 Thessalonians 4:17, *"Then we which are alive* and *remain shall be caught up together with them in the clouds, to meet the Lord in the air: and so shall we ever be with the Lord."*

1 Corinthians 15:51, ***"Behold, I shew you a mystery;*** *We shall not all sleep, but we shall all be changed".*

Over the years I have studied the Bible with the view of knowing God and understanding the truth. I have witnessed denominational Churches formed and some eventually collapsed. The subject of Rapture, remains extremely sensitive and controversial among believers. Various divergent views on this subject have even caused divisions and doctrinal conflicts among Churches.

With this background I am impressed to explain briefly on the resurrection of the dead and the **doctrine of Rapture**. As a scholar, I have discovered in my research that in the Greek New Testament there are three words mentioned in connection with the second coming of Christ. The *apocalypses* which means unveiling, *epiphanenia* which means the appearing and **parousia** which means the Lord's presence, the personal presence alongside. These terms are to some extend used interchangeably but in the preponderance of instances it is the term parousia which is employed to designate the Rapture. The word, Rapture itself, like the word Trinity does not appear in the New English Testament but the thought of rapture is there. This word is used by most Christians, means to be taken away or to be "caught up". In 1 Thessalonians 4:17, *"Then we which are alive and remain shall be caught up together with them in the clouds, to meet the Lord in the air: and so shall we ever be with the Lord."*

I believe the Holy life for the church life is a life with a future, a life with hope. This hope is not merely the Lord's coming; it is the

Lord's coming with resurrection and rapture. The Lord's coming back will cause resurrection and rapture to occur. It is important to know that resurrection and rapture are both addition to life. Resurrection, of course, is for those who have died. Today we are living a holy life for the church. If the Lord delays His coming back we shall eventually "sleep" that is die physically. All the believers who have died are awaiting resurrection. If we live until the coming back of the Lord Jesus, we shall not need resurrection. However we shall still need rapture. Furthermore, those who have died will need to be resurrected and raptured as well. All believers the dead as well as the living need rapture, this is the hope we have in Christ. I believe in the Rapture, the whole Church, the risen dead and the remaining living will for the first time in history, be on the move together.

No mortality - "*The dead in Christ shall rise*". For the trumpet shall sound and the dead shall be raised.

1 Corinthians 15:52. No inquiry haunts the human heart so poignantly as the inquiry as to where are the dead. Just imagine someone has died in a room, in a house, no door and no window opened but there is no doubt that he is gone. The philosophical question is "gone where exactly". This is mystery, for we know in part (Deuteronomy 29:29). It is however appropriate here to point out that Christian doctrine teaches not only the immortality of soul but the resurrection of the body. I believe that God created man to be immortal and made him to be an image for eternity the New Jerusalem which is choegraphically prophesied in the book of Revelation by Apostle John the Revelator. When our Lord triumphed over death, it was not just His Spirit that survived, it was His total personality and at Rapture there will be not only a reunion of spirits but a resurrection of the bodies of the faithful saints. "*That which thou sowest, thou sowest not the body that shall be, but bare grain. It may be a chance of wheat or of some other grain, but God giveth it a body; as it hath pleased Him and every seed his own body*"

1 Corinthians 15:37, 38. 1 Corinthians 15:52, "*For the trumpet shall sound, and the dead shall be raised incorruptible.*" "*The dead in*

Christ shall rise" 1 Thessalonians 4:16. Isaiah 26:19, "Thy dead *men* shall live, *together with* my dead body shall they arise. Awake and sing, ye that dwell in dust: for thy dew *is as* the dew of herbs, and the earth shall cast out the dead." Acts 26:8, "Why should it be thought a thing incredible with you, that God should raise the dead?"

There has been a heated theological debate on the destination or whereabouts of a person who dies. Some may say when saints die, they go to heaven and when the Lord Jesus comes back, He will bring them from heaven with Him. To interpret the verse in this way is to neglect the first half of the verse where we are told that Jesus died and rose. This, of course, refers to His resurrection. If the dead saints are already in heaven and the Lord will bring them with Him from heaven when He comes, then the dead saints do not need resurrection. This is definitely an interesting theological debate for an edition.

1 Thessalonians 4:15-16, *"For this we say unto you by the word of the Lord, that we which are alive* and *remain unto the coming of the Lord shall not prevent them which are asleep. For the Lord himself shall descend from heaven with a shout, with the voice of the archangel, and with the trump of God: and the dead in Christ shall rise first"*. This verse will help us understand this subject. Please pay close attention to the word *"rise"*. If the dead are already in heaven what need is there for them to rise? If they are truly in heaven they do not need to rise. Furthermore they do not need to be raptured or to be caught up to the Lord. Their only need would be to descend from heaven with the Lord Jesus. The fact that verse 16 says that the dead in Christ shall rise indicates that they must be in some other place not heaven. We need to get rid of the "heavenly mansion" theology. I am fully convinced that the dead in Christ go to paradise and when the Lord Jesus comes, they will rise up. This is not rise up to heaven rather they will rise up and then be caught up together with the living saints. This is the reason verse 16 says that the dead in Christ shall rise first. According to the word of God, when the Lord Jesus descends from heaven, the dead saints will rise up. Their spirit and

soul will rise out of paradise. Their body will rise up from the tomb and their spirit and soul with body will make them perfect. Then will join the believers who are living and together we shall all be caught up to the Lord. Agreeably, we might doctrinally differ on this subject but the fundamental focus is that of keeping the unity of the faith in Christ, this should be maintained non-negotiably.

Be focussed do not lose sight of the ultimate

We see Bible prophecy is like a jigsaw puzzle. As we navigate scriptures we see prophecy upon prophecy fulfilled with precision and divine accuracy. **Dr Duncan Malveren said, *"We can have the party and enjoy but we should not lose the focus on the purpose of the party."*** This statement is contextually relevant to believers on earth awaiting for the coming of the Lord. The inference is that we can have what we have to enjoy on earth but our primary focus should be to please God the Father. We must undeniably and unquestionably express Him to the lost humanity and to be the epitome of His perfect representation on the earth. Luke 18:18 *"....Nevertheless when the Son of Man cometh shall he find faith on the earth?"* Here Jesus was not talking of faith we are taught in our denominational Churches, the faith to claim things for material prosperity, or the faith for breakthroughs etc. ***He is talking of His substance, essence, reality, influence, His universal impact and accurate representation on the earth.**** The expression of His glory. Christ's concern is to see the "deposit" of Himself in His creation on His return. This is the substance which constitute His Church and is the substance which is used to construct His Kingdom on the earth. Christ's primary divine objective is to set up a Kingdom not a religious institution characterised by ceremonial laws, endless and unachievable regulations. Simply, Jesus came to set up a government for God, a ruler-ship over heaven and earth. In practical reality, Christ's mandate was and still is to establish a Kingdom with a universal jurisdiction over God's all creation. Daniel 2:44, *"And in the days of these Kings shall* **the God of heaven set up a Kingdom,** *which shall never be destroyed: and the Kingdom shall not be left to other people,* but *it shall break in pieces and consume all these kingdoms, and it shall stand for ever."* We should not be like them who fail away into perdition because of the deceit and craftiness of Satan. There are multitudes who have fallen into apostasy (apostasia) 1 Timothy 4:1. All events in the earth are progressively moving towards the closing of this age. This is the word of God expressed. Therefore, we should take heed and be alert.

The Holy Spirit is moulding the grand universal and corporate temple of God on earth in fulfilment of Jesus prayer, *"Thy Kingdom Come"*. I believe we are the finishing generation and the finished work of Christ will never be fully manifested without us. All those who died in the faith without having received what was promised will not be made perfect. We are the corporate man who has to cross triumphantly and victoriously to the finishing line. The restoration of all things spoken by the prophets of the old will be first fulfilled in His grand return. This is the universal celebration of the closing of an age and entering into another eternal age.

Watchfulness of His return

In our study of the bible we have discovered that prophecy of Kingdom concern the Church and the Lord persistently admonish us to be watchful and prudent as we await His coming back. We should not lose sight and focus of the Kingdom. The Kingdom is God's eternal purpose even before the foundation of the world. Luke 12:32 *"Fear not, little flock; for it is your Father's good pleasure to give you the Kingdom."* If there is anything in the heart of our eternal God, is the matter concerning the Kingdom which is practically HIS HABITATION THE NEW JERUSALEM, the total fulfilment of the FEAST OF TABERNACLES.

Obadiah 1:17, *".......; and the house of Jacob shall possess their possessions."* Our possession is His Kingdom. We need to rise up, participate and be watchful as Christ is gathering nations for God to bring to an end this age.

The enemy of God is constantly, tirelessly and intransigently mobilizing his forces to destabilise the agenda of Christ on the earth.

In the parabolic teachings of the Lord in the Gospels several scriptures have been given as an admonition against religious complacency, laxity, passivity, mediocrity and general slothfulness. But Matthew 25:1-13 gives us a striking teaching example on watchfulness and readiness. Verse 1; *"Then shall the Kingdom of heaven be likened unto ten virgins, which took their lamps, and went forth to meet the bridegroom."* The word "Then" here means "at that time" that is at the time of the parousia. When the parousia described in the Pauline epistles take place, the Lord warned, many things will happen. Then the Kingdom of God will be likened to ten virgins. Virgins signify believers in the aspect of Church life.

Believers are the Kingdom people, like chaste virgins bearing the Lord's testimony (the lamp) in the dark age and going out of the world to meet the Lord. We see for this they need not only the indwelling but also the fullness of the Spirit of God. Verse 1 says, the virgins took their lamps and went forth to meet the bridegroom. Lamps also signify the spirit of believers (Proverbs 20:27) which contains the Spirit of God as oil. (Romans 8:16) The believers shine with light of the Spirit of God from within their spirit. Thus they become the light of the world like a lamp shining in the darkness of this age. (Mathew 5:14-16) (Philippians 2:15-16) to bear the testimony of the Lord for the glorification of God. We need to be people of the word so we will be assured of a triumphant entry into the Kingdom to come, the total fulfilment of the final feast, the feast of the Tabernacles. The reality of the restoration of all things in Christ and the establishment of his final Kingdom.

<u>The enduring faith</u>

In this journey towards the finish we need not depart from the central focus of the life of Christ. There is also urgency in the demonic kingdom of the Devil to accelerate his wicked machinations to counter the advancement of the Kingdom of Christ. One preacher known for teaching on spiritual welfare once said. **"As the consummation of the age become more and more of a reality. The battle increasingly becomes more ferocious and deadlier."** I believe this is a true practical reality of an insight in the realm of the spirit.

As New Testament Ministers of the Gospel we may need to add another dimension of truth which has been since neglected by most believers in their walk of faith, the teaching of the enduring faith. As believers we need to constantly conscious of the possibility of suffering and persecution as we follow Christ. The church has to teach people that the "milk and honey Canaan land" theology is not real and it revolts against biblical teaching on carrying our cross as we follow Christ. We cannot completely rule out the possibility of suffering in this life though we believe in God and have faith in Christ. The truth is we need to partner with God in dealing with our detractors as we fight to possess our inheritance. Joshua 3:10, *"And Joshua said, Hereby ye shall know that the living God is among you, and that he will without fail drive out from before you the Canaanites, and the Hittites, and the Hivites, and the Perizzites, and the Girgashites, and the Amorites, and the Jebusites."* **We have no promise for a "battle-free" life in this world but our Lord Jesus has promised us victory in Him**. John 16:33, *".....In the world ye shall have tribulation but be of good cheer, I have overcome the world."* Believers in this Christ at some point definitely go through dark seasons or cycles of life. Time and time again there is contrary wind. But in Christ we prevail and in Him we are positioned for victory. There is always opposition and sometimes ferocious opposition. But our Lord promised us victory. Believers have to be taught on persecution, suffering, endurance, patience and tribulation as we follow Christ. **Being born again does not exonerate one from these experiences sometimes even unavoidable wilderness experiences.** If we do not go through these how then is the scripture going to be fulfilled? Matthew 26:54, *"But how then shall the scriptures be fulfilled, that thus it must be?"*

A lot of negative experiences we go through sometimes might even bring us into maturity and perfection as we witness the fulfilment of scriptures. For the fulfilment of scriptures is the manifestation of the glory of God. Let me unhesitatingly emphasise that the "all weather, prosperous and trouble-free gospel" is not all truth and not real. If I had space I would have quoted innumerable scriptures in support of this argument.

The great Apostle Paul in 2 Corinthians 11:24-33 (you can read all) gives us a historical account of his experiences. Among us, apart from our Lord Jesus Christ, who can be greater than Paul the Apostle? In fact, in some portion of scriptures he says, *"I boast in infirmities"*. The Psalmist in Psalms 119:50, *"This is my comfort in my affliction: for thy word hath quickened me."* I find comfort in afflictions. We need the Church to teach the believers more on the enduring faith. (Romans 5:1-5). Another striking example of scripture is 2 Timothy 2:3, *"**Thou therefore endure hardness**, as a good soldier of Jesus Christ."* And on verse 10 we hear the Apostle stating, *"Wherein I suffer trouble......"* For clarity, it must be noted that I am not advocating for the "theology of suffering". There is a suffering which comes as a result of ignorance, and blatant disobedience to the guidance of the Holy Spirit and the Holy Word of God. I am talking about enduring the cross in His Will and purpose.

We need to believe God for the constant activation of the Holy Spirit in us. Ephesians 3:16; *".....to be strengthened with might by His Spirit in the inner man."* The Holy Spirit is the "dynamo" inside us and He assures us victory and provides timeous revelation in dealing with these forces of darkness. **We need to endure to the end. Jesus**

Christ our Lord is coming and we need to hold on faith; we need to be part of the grand universal celebration to come.

We thank God for the provision of the Holy Spirit we always have insights in the unfolding events in this age and the age to come. The Holy Ghost sets a distinct trajectory in our journey towards the fulfilment of God's purpose. Let us open our spiritual ears (the Spirit) as we connect to the frequency from the realm of our Father. Among the children of Israel, apart from the tribe of Judah, there was another tribe I always want to relate to. This is the tribe of Issachar, the Sons of Issachar had the spiritual capacity to discern the times. Actually, the bible says they *knew what Israel ought to do.* (1 Chronicle 12:32). It is always power and strength to know and have an understanding of what God wants to do. The activated Spirit of discernment is our spiritual compass. We should not be ignorant of the dynamics of the Spirit realm. Like Apostle Paul echoed in 1 Corinthians 9:26, *"I therefore so run, not as uncertainly; so fight I, not as one that beateth the air:"* We are not supposed to run and walk in darkness and fight in blindness. The Devil will not win and will never win in this battle for our God reigns. Psalm 97 *"....The Lord reigneth...."* He is on the unshakeble throne. **GLORY, GLORY, TO THE LAMB OF GOD IN THE HIGHEST AMEN, AMEN**

Printed in the United States
By Bookmasters